JOURNEYS

Reader's Notebook

Volume 1

Grade 3

Printed in the U.S.A.

ISBN 978-0-547-86065-7

33 34 35 36 0928 21 20

4500807444 B C D E F G

Contents

Name ______________________ Date ____________

Words with Short Vowels

A Fine, Fine School
Phonics:
Short Vowels *a, e, i, o, u*

Read each word. Then find and circle it in the Word Find. Words can go across or down.

gentle	empty	visit	lily
softly	glance	puppy	tumble

s	o	v	t	l	y	u	s	o
p	v	i	s	i	t	s	o	y
u	i	l	o	g	u	f	f	s
p	s	y	f	e	m	p	t	y
p	g	l	a	n	c	e	l	t
y	l	i	e	t	u	m	y	o
p	u	l	m	l	i	l	e	s
t	u	y	p	e	m	y	l	y
b	m	u	t	u	m	b	l	e

Write each word in the correct place in the chart below.

Words with Short Vowels

a	e	i	o	u

Name ________________________ Date ____________

The Subject of a Simple Sentence

- A sentence is a group of words that tells a complete thought. The **subject** of a simple sentence tells whom or what the sentence is about.
- The subject usually comes at the beginning of the sentence. The subject can be one word or more than one word. The **complete subject** includes all the words in the subject.

  The weekend is a special time.

  My family enjoys the holidays.

Thinking Question
Whom or what is the sentence about?

Write the complete subject of each simple sentence.

1. Saturday is a fun day. ____________
2. All my friends get together in the park. ____________
3. Baseball teams play on the fields. ____________
4. My father coaches the teams. ____________
5. My mother watches all the games. ____________
6. Our neighbors bring lots of food. ____________
7. We cook outside until it is dark. ____________
8. The kids sleep on a blanket. ____________
9. Grandma and Grandpa tell stories. ____________
10. Many of our teachers join us. ____________

Name ____________________ Date __________

The Predicate of a Simple Sentence

- Every simple sentence has two parts—the subject and the predicate.
- The **predicate** is the part of a sentence that tells what the subject does or is.
- The predicate can be one word or more than one word. The **complete predicate** includes all the words in the predicate.

  I lie beside the river.

  My body relaxes in the sun.

Thinking Question
Which word or words in the sentence tell what the subject does or is?

Write each sentence. Then underline the complete predicate.

1. Relaxing is not as easy as it looks.

   ____

2. I like to watch the clouds above me.

   ____

3. Gerry enjoys floating in the pool.

   ____

4. Ernie sits on the back steps with his dog.

   ____

5. My cousins swing in tires hung from ropes.

   ____

Name ______________________ Date ______________

A Fine, Fine School
Spelling:
Short Vowels

Spelling Word Sort

Write each Basic Word under the correct heading. One word will go under two different headings.

Short *a*	Short *e*
______	______
______	______
______	______
Short *i*	**Short *o***
______	______
______	______
______	______
______	**Short *u***
______	______
______	______
______	______
______	______

Spelling Words

Basic

1. crop
2. plan
3. thing
4. smell
5. shut
6. sticky
7. spent
8. lunch
9. pumpkin
10. clock
11. gift
12. class
13. skip
14. swing

Review

next
hug

Challenge

hospital
fantastic

Review: **Add the Review Words to your Word Sort.**

Challenge: Which Challenge Word has short vowels *o* and *i*?

____

Name ______________________ Date __________

Focus Trait: Word Choice

Exact Words

Without Exact Words	With Exact Words
Mr. Brown lived in a big house.	Mr. Brown lived in the enormous, old green mansion on the hill, behind Taft Middle School.

A. Read the sentence that does not use exact words. Then choose words and add details to make the description more exact.

Without Exact Words	With Exact Words
1. Every day I go to school.	Every ______________ I ____________ to ______________________.

B. Read each sentence that does not use exact words. Then look at the illustration on pages 26–27 of *A Fine, Fine School*. Rewrite the sentence using exact words.

Pair/Share **Work with a partner to brainstorm exact words to use.**

Without Exact Words	With Exact Words
2. The children are staying busy.	
3. Mr. Keene is making a face.	
4. The children are using their lockers.	

Name ________________________ Date ____________

Words with the VCCV Pattern

Write a word from the box to complete each sentence in the story.

basket	happened	suddenly
chipmunk	princess	garden
rabbit	puppet	trumpet
galloped		

1. The blaring ____________ announced the show would soon begin.
2. Children sat in front of a little stage in the ____________.
3. Everyone was excited to see the ____________ show.
4. A furry ____________ was the first puppet onstage.
5. Next came a little ____________ puppet.
6. What ____________ next was a surprise.
7. The rabbit told the chipmunk she was really a beautiful ____________.
8. The chipmunk gave the rabbit a ____________ of flowers.
9. The rabbit ____________ disappeared, and a beautiful princess stood in her place.
10. The princess and the chipmunk ____________ away on a horse.

Name ______________________ Date ______

A Fine, Fine School

The Fine, Fine School Times

Tillie is writing an article for the school newspaper, *The Fine, Fine School Times*. Her article will tell the real story. Use the text and illustrations to help her write the article.

Read pages 20–23. How do the students and teachers feel about going to school on the weekends and during the summer?

Mr. Keene just announced school will be open every single day of the year. I talked to some students and teachers. The students feel that ______________________

____

The teachers are worried that they might ____________

____

Mr. Keene has a different opinion. He thinks that the teachers and students will love coming to school every day because ______________________

____

That's all the news for now!

Name ______________________ Date ______

Read pages 30–33. Now Mr. Keene has changed his mind about keeping school open every day. Tillie has written another article to share the news.

The big news in school today is that school will be closed on weekends and during the summer. Mr. Keene said that the main reason for the change was

____

____

I talked to some students about the change. One student told me that she liked the days off because

____

____

Another student told me that now when he was not in school he could learn other things, like ____________

____

The teachers and students are all pleased with Mr. Keene's decision. That is all the news for now from *The Fine, Fine School Times.*

Name ______________________ Date __________

Lesson 1
READER'S NOTEBOOK

A Fine, Fine School
Grammar:
Simple Sentences

Sentence Fragments

Write the complete subject of each simple sentence. Then underline the complete predicate.

1. Ira loves to read books in summer. ______________________
2. Gina helps her dad all summer. ______________________
3. Michaela rides her bike. ______________________
4. Wanda and Jane planted a garden. ______________________
5. The kids on Roy's block play baseball. ______________________

Write a complete simple sentence for each sentence fragment.

6. Tera and her swim team.

   ____

7. Has games all summer.

   ____

8. Have frozen treats.

   ____

9. My friend.

   ____

10. In the car.

   ____

Name ______________________ Date ____________

Short Vowels

Write a Basic Word to finish the second sentence in each pair of sentences.

1. Water is wet.

   Glue is ______________.
2. You eat breakfast in the morning.

   You eat ______________ at noon.
3. You use a ruler to measure length.

   You use a ______________ to measure time.
4. You see with your eyes.

   You ______________ with your nose.
5. A writer writes a book.

   A farmer plants a ______________.
6. You can earn money by doing a job.

   When your money is gone, it is ______________.
7. Watermelons are seen in summer.

   ______________ are seen in fall.
8. A wolf is part of a pack.

   A student is part of a ______________.
9. A horse learns to prance.

   A child learns to ______________.
10. Before you enter, you must open a door.

    When you leave, you ______________ the door.

Challenge: Make up a pair of sentences similar to the ones above. Use a Challenge Word as the answer.

Spelling Words

Basic

1. crop
2. plan
3. thing
4. smell
5. shut
6. sticky
7. spent
8. lunch
9. pumpkin
10. clock
11. gift
12. class
13. skip
14. swing

Review

next
hug

Challenge

hospital
fantastic

Name ______________________ Date ____________

Context Clues

A Fine, Fine School
Vocabulary Strategies:
Context Clues

Read the sentence. Write the meaning of the underlined word as it is used in the sentence. Use a dictionary if you need help.

1. One <u>fine</u> day when the weather was nice, our family went on a picnic.

____

2. We ate sandwiches and tried a new <u>kind</u> of juice drink.

____

3. We plan to take another <u>trip</u> to the park soon.

____

4. Elena was <u>fatigued</u> after the long, busy day.

____

5. The <u>immense</u> sign blocked our view of the building.

____

6. The winter day is too <u>frigid</u> to go outdoors.

____

7. Jeffrey was so surprised at what he saw, he couldn't stop <u>gaping</u>.

____

8. The detective had a <u>crucial</u> piece of information about the theft.

____

Name ______________________ Date ____________

Lesson 1
READER'S NOTEBOOK

A Fine, Fine School
Grammar:
Spiral Review

Capitalization and Punctuation

- Correct **capitalization** includes capitalizing the first letter of sentences.
- Every sentence has end **punctuation**, such as a period.

My pencil needs to be sharpened.

Now my writing will be easy to read.

Write each sentence using correct capitalization and punctuation.

1. our school principal visited our class today

____

2. all students will take the test next week

____

3. the math teacher surprised all of us

____

4. that is my favorite book

____

5. today is a holiday

____

6. i saw Mr. Clarke yesterday

____

Name ______________________ Date __________

Proofreading for Spelling

Read the following invitation. Find and circle the misspelled words.

You're Invited!

Please plen to attend Mr. Hay's cless next Monday.

We have spint three weeks learning about autumn. We want to share some of the thangs we learned with you.

We will begin when the cluck strikes ten. We will shet the doors at that time. We will teach you about some crups farmers grow in our area in the fall. Then we will discuss interesting facts about the sun and Earth at this time of year. Finally, we will eat. You will be hungry from the delicious smill of pompken pie! It will be our gaft to you.

Write the misspelled words correctly on the lines below.

1. ______________ 6. ______________

2. ______________ 7. ______________

3. ______________ 8. ______________

4. ______________ 9. ______________

5. ______________ 10. ______________

Spelling Words

Basic

1. crop
2. plan
3. thing
4. smell
5. shut
6. sticky
7. spent
8. lunch
9. pumpkin
10. clock
11. gift
12. class
13. skip
14. swing

Review

next
hug

Challenge

hospital
fantastic

Name ______________________ Date ____________

Connect to Writing

Sometimes a sentence does not include a complete thought. It is a **fragment**. Correct fragments by adding the missing subject or predicate. This will make your writing easier to understand.

Fragments	Complete Simple Sentences
Taught our cat to fetch. Raul taught.	Raul taught our cat to fetch.
My sister. Showed the puppy tricks.	My sister showed the puppy tricks.

Correct the fragments by combining the subjects and predicates to form complete simple sentences. Write the sentence on the line.

1. Our dog. Loves bones.

   ____

2. Grandpa a trick. Taught him a trick.

   ____

3. Dogs attention. Love attention.

   ____

4. Danny taught. Our dog to sit.

   ____

5. The dog to come. Begged us to come.

   ____

Name ______________________ Date ______________

Words with Long Vowels

The Trial of Cardigan Jones
Phonics:
Long Vowels *a, e, i, o, u*

Read each clue. Write two rhyming words from the Word Bank to answer the clue.

base	rage	globe	joke
home	shade	skate	lime
broke	chase	plate	tone
robe	chrome	slime	phone
cage	shake	snake	trade

1. If you chase your friend around the bases on a field, you play a game of ______________ ______________.

2. If a joke wasn't funny, the ______________ ______________.

3. If a lime rots, you will have ______________ ______________.

4. A snake that is cold does a ______________ ______________.

5. An angry bird in a cage may get ______________ ______________.

6. If you put paper plates under your feet, you can go for a ______________ ______________.

7. If you put on a bathrobe with a round map of the world on it, you are wearing a ______________ ______________.

8. If you switch shady spots, you do a ______________ ______________.

9. When you pick up a telephone, you hear a sound called a ______________ ______________.

10. A shiny, silver house is a ______________ ______________.

Name ______________________ Date ____________

Statements and Questions

- Every sentence begins with a capital letter. There are four kinds of sentences. Statements and questions are two of them.
- A sentence that tells something is a **statement**. It ends with a period. It is also called a **declarative** sentence.
- A sentence that asks something is a **question**. It ends with a question mark. It is also called an **interrogative** sentence.

Statement/Declarative
I wear comfortable clothes.

Question/Interrogative
What do you like to wear?

Thinking Question
Is the sentence a statement or a question, and how do I know?

Write *statement* if the sentence tells something. Write *question* if the sentence asks something.

1. I wear old shirts around the house. ______________
2. Why don't you go and change your clothes? ______________
3. Who is coming to visit? ______________
4. I dress up for company. ______________
5. Why do my old clothes feel so good? ______________
6. Old cotton shirts are very soft. ______________
7. A new dress can feel strange. ______________
8. My pet moves around the house. ______________

Name ______________________ Date ____________

Commands and Exclamations

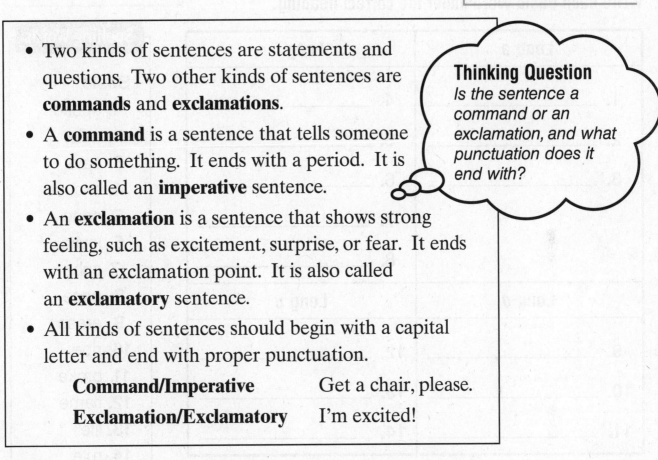

- Two kinds of sentences are statements and questions. Two other kinds of sentences are **commands** and **exclamations**.
- A **command** is a sentence that tells someone to do something. It ends with a period. It is also called an **imperative** sentence.
- An **exclamation** is a sentence that shows strong feeling, such as excitement, surprise, or fear. It ends with an exclamation point. It is also called an **exclamatory** sentence.
- All kinds of sentences should begin with a capital letter and end with proper punctuation.

Command/Imperative	Get a chair, please.
Exclamation/Exclamatory	I'm excited!

Thinking Question
Is the sentence a command or an exclamation, and what punctuation does it end with?

Write *command* if the sentence tells someone to do something. Write *exclamation* if the sentence shows strong feeling.

1. That is the funniest joke! ______________
2. Tell another joke. ______________
3. I am so happy! ______________
4. Bring everyone in to hear these. ______________
5. How my sides hurt from laughing! ______________
6. Pull out those chairs and sit down. ______________
7. Please repeat that joke. ______________

Name ______________________ Date ____________

Spelling Word Sort

The Trial of Cardigan Jones
Spelling:
VC*e* Spellings

Write each Basic Word under the correct heading.

Long *a*	Long *i*
1. ________	4. ________
2. ________	5. ________
3. ________	6. ________
	7. ________
	8. ________
Long *o*	**Long *u***
9. ________	12. ________
10. ________	13. ________
11. ________	14. ________

Review: What long vowel sound does the Review Word *these* have? ____________ What long vowel sound does the Review Word *those* have? ____________

Challenge: In which column do the two Challenge Words belong? ____________

Spelling Words

Basic
1. spoke
2. mile
3. save
4. excuse
5. cone
6. invite
7. cube
8. price
9. erase
10. ripe
11. broke
12. flame
13. life
14. rule

Review
these
those

Challenge
surprise
decide

Name ______________________ Date __________

Lesson 2
READER'S NOTEBOOK

The Trial of Cardigan Jones
Writing: Narrative Writing

Focus Trait: Ideas

Audience and Purpose

Without Interesting Details	With Interesting Details
The milkman told the judge what he saw.	"Judge, I'm sure I saw the moose tiptoe up to the window and put his face right into the pie" said the milkman.

A. Read the sentence below. Rewrite the sentence with more interesting details and dialogue to entertain your audience.

Without Interesting Details	With Interesting Details
1. The moose was clumsy.	

B. Read each sentence below. Rewrite the sentences, adding details and dialogue that will make each one more interesting to the reader.

Pair/Share **Work with a partner to find details to add to the sentences.**

Without Interesting Details	With Interesting Details
2. Page 54: Mrs. Brown didn't know what happened to her pie.	
3. Page 66: The judge found the missing pie.	

Words with the VC*e* Pattern

Read each word. Draw a line to match the word to its meaning.

Column 1	Column 2
1. awake	a. clothes worn to make somebody look like somebody or something else
2. costume	b. to free oneself or get away from
3. divide	c. to bring things together
4. escape	d. an error
5. exercise	e. not asleep
6. microphone	f. a paved path where people can walk alongside a street
7. mistake	g. to separate
8. refuse	h. to say no
9. sidewalk	i. to work out or do a physical activity
10. unite	j. a device to make someone's voice louder

Write each word from Column 1 in the correct place in the chart below. Look at the part of the word with the VC*e* pattern.

Long *a*	Long *i*	Long *o*	Long *u*

Name ______________________ Date ______

The Trial of Cardigan Jones

Questions for the Milkman

What would you say if you were the milkman? Right now, the judge is asking you questions about Cardigan Jones. Use the text and illustrations to explain exactly what you saw that day.

Read page 53.

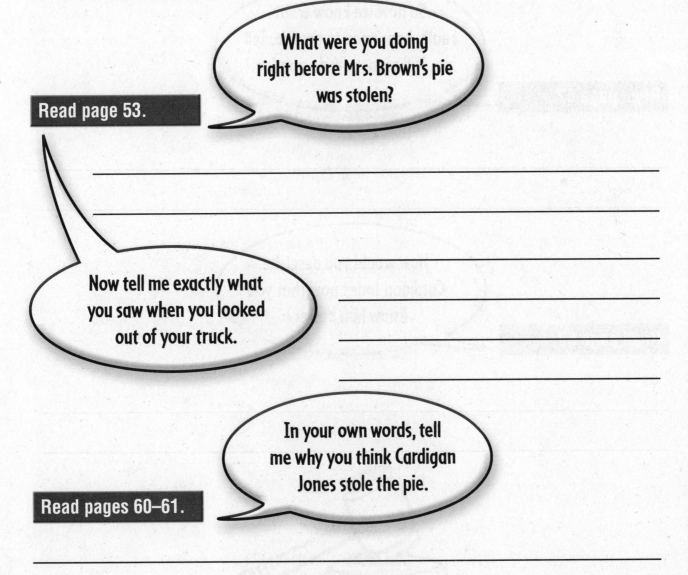

What were you doing right before Mrs. Brown's pie was stolen?

____

____

Now tell me exactly what you saw when you looked out of your truck.

____

____

____

____

Read pages 60–61.

In your own words, tell me why you think Cardigan Jones stole the pie.

____

____

Name ______________________________ Date ______

The Trial of Cardigan Jones
Independent Reading

Read page 62.

What have you observed about Cardigan Jones in this courtroom?

____

____

Read page 67.

So now we know what really happened to the pie. Tell me, Milkman, how do you feel?

____

____

Read page 69.

How would you describe Cardigan Jones now that you know him better?

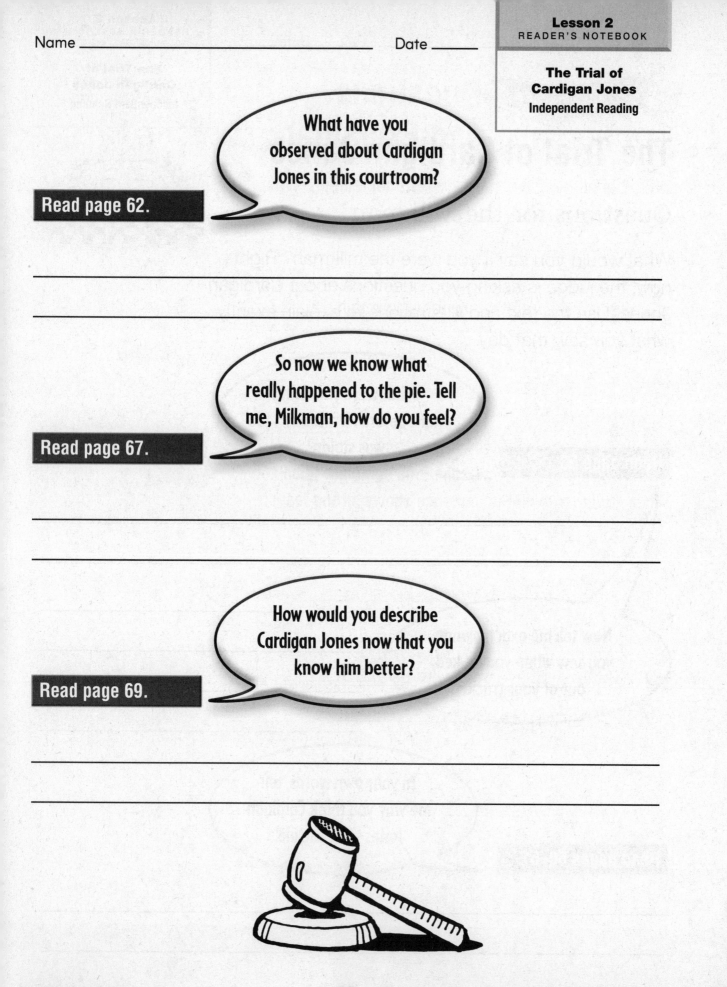

____

____

Name ______________________ Date ____________

Statements, Questions, Commands, and Exclamations

Write *statement* if the sentence tells something. Write *question* if the sentence asks something.

1. I like basketball. ____________

2. I would not want to climb a mountain. ____________

3. Where do you row your boat? ____________

4. Do you like to play tennis? ____________

5. What do you know about judo? ____________

Write *command* if the sentence tells someone to do something. Write *exclamation* if the sentence shows strong feeling.

6. Pick up the tennis racket. ____________

7. Tennis is a great sport! ____________

8. Please join me in a game. ____________

9. Ask him to play tennis with us. ____________

10. I will not ask him! ____________

Name ______________________ Date ____________

VC*e* Spellings

Write the Basic Word that belongs in each group.

1. sphere, pyramid, ______________,
____
2. fire, smoke, ______________
3. inch, yard, ______________
4. ask, call, ______________
5. ready, full-grown, ______________
6. whispered, yelled, ______________
7. law, principle, ______________
8. change, wipe away, ______________
9. rescue, free, ______________
10. amount, cost, ______________

Challenge: Which Challenge Word belongs in a group called *Things That Are Unexpected*? ______________

Spelling Words

Basic
1. spoke
2. mile
3. save
4. excuse
5. cone
6. invite
7. cube
8. price
9. erase
10. ripe
11. broke
12. flame
13. life
14. rule

Review
these
those

Challenge
surprise
decide

Name ______________________ Date __________

Dictionary/Glossary

Read each word. Find each word in a dictionary or glossary. Complete the chart.

Word	Part(s) of Speech	Word with Endings
1. gavel		
2. pilfer		
3. declare		
4. testify		
5. fine		

Now write one sentence of your own that could be an example sentence for one meaning of each word.

1. ______________________________

2. ______________________________

3. ______________________________

4. ______________________________

5. ______________________________

Name ______________________ Date ____________

Writing Subjects and Predicates

- The **subject** of a sentence tells whom or what the sentence is about. The main word in a sentence is often a **noun**. It is called the **simple subject**.
- The **predicate** of a sentence tells what the subject is or was, or what the subject does or did. The main word in the predicate is a **verb**. It is called the **simple predicate**.

The complete subject of each sentence is underlined. Write the simple subject.

1. The room for the dance was large. ______________
2. The band's first song had a fast tempo. ______________
3. The twins said they would dance to every song. ______________
4. The girl in the yellow dress danced happily. ______________

The complete predicate of each sentence is underlined. Write the simple predicate.

5. The teachers put drinks and snacks on the tables. ______________
6. I looked for my cousin on the dance floor. ______________
7. Everyone danced to the last song. ______________
8. The tired dancers walked home happy. ______________

Lesson 2
READER'S NOTEBOOK

Name ______________________ Date ____________

Proofreading for Spelling

The Trial of Cardigan Jones
Spelling:
VC*e* Spellings

Read the following passage. Find and circle the misspelled words.

Do you sometimes wish there was no such thing as a roole? Let's think about how lief would be different without rules. You may surpris yourself and be thankful for rules!

Let's say you have an ice cream con. I see it and decid I want it. I take your ice cream. I do not say excoose me. I eat it all, even though you paid the prise for it.

Thos actions would make you mad, wouldn't they? But since there are no rules, the only thing I brok was your pride. I did not break a rule.

Rules saav us from situations like these. Rules help us all get along.

Spelling Words

Basic
1. spoke
2. mile
3. save
4. excuse
5. cone
6. invite
7. cube
8. price
9. erase
10. ripe
11. broke
12. flame
13. life
14. rule

Review
these
those

Challenge
surprise
decide

Write the misspelled words correctly on the lines below.

1. ____________ 6. ____________
2. ____________ 7. ____________
3. ____________ 8. ____________
4. ____________ 9. ____________
5. ____________ 10. ____________

Name ______________________ Date __________

Connect to Writing

Sentences can be statements, questions, commands, or exclamations. Using all four kinds of sentences in a paragraph makes writing more lively and varied.

Paragraph with One Kind of Sentence	Paragraph with Four Kinds of Sentences
Rowing a boat can be lots of fun. You should try it. You find a boat. You will laugh a lot.	Rowing a boat can be lots of fun. Why don't you try it? Find a boat. You will not stop laughing!

Change each sentence to another type of sentence. The word in parentheses tells you the type of sentence to write. Write the new sentence on the line.

1. We won the boat race. (exclamation)

____

2. Do you row the boats there? (statement)

____

3. Can we put this boat in the water? (command)

____

4. We should watch the boat race. (question)

____

5. Will you let me ride in the boat? (statement)

____

Name ______________________ Date ____________

Destiny's Gift
Phonics: Common Vowel Pairs
ai, ay, ee, ea

Common Vowel Pairs *ai, ay, ee, ea*

Write the word from the Word Bank that best completes each sentence.

always	easel	stain	steam
bait	greedy	players	sweeten
breeze	rain	queen	trail
chain	layers	seasons	

1. Of all the ______________, fall is my favorite.
2. When you boil water, the ______________ you see is the water vapor.
3. Take your umbrella because it will ______________.
4. The door is secured with a lock and strong ______________.
5. I knew it was the ______________ because of her crown.
6. The hikers walked along the marked ______________.
7. The artist paints at his ______________.
8. To be safe, I ______________ look both ways at a stop sign.
9. I will use honey to ______________ the iced tea.
10. The cake has three different ______________.
11. The spilled juice left a ______________ on the carpet.
12. On a hot day, a ______________ is welcome.
13. Remember to take the ______________ with you when you go fishing.
14. Four ______________ can play the game at the same time.
15. If you do not share, people may think you are ______________.

Name ______________________ Date __________

Simple and Compound Sentences

- A **simple sentence** tells a complete thought.
- A **compound sentence** is made up of two simple sentences joined by the word *and*, *but*, *or*, or *so*.

  We stood in the front yard. Our neighbors stayed indoors.

  We stood in the front yard, but our neighbors stayed indoors.

Thinking Question
Does the sentence tell one complete thought, or does it tell two complete thoughts?

Determine whether each sentence is simple or compound. Write *simple* or *compound* on the line.

1. Young students and their friends met at the bookstore.

   ____

2. The children handed out flyers, and their parents carried signs. ______________________

3. A large group of people shouted, but they were not angry.

   ____

4. They shouted to get people to come to the bookstore.

   ____

5. Many old customers came, and some customers gave speeches. ______________________

6. People could buy books, or they could donate money.

   ____

Name ____________________ Date __________

Coordinating Conjunctions

- A **compound sentence** is made up of two simple sentences joined by a conjunction.
- The words *and*, *but*, *or*, and *so* are **conjunctions**. A comma comes before the conjunction.

  And joins two similar ideas.

  But joins two different ideas.

  Or joins two possible ideas.

  So shows that the second idea happens because of the first.

Thinking Question
Which kinds of ideas are being joined into one sentence?

Write the conjunction that best joins the simple sentences. Then write the compound sentence.

1. Dora called Lisa. She called Erin.

____

____

2. Erin was at home. Lisa was not at home.

____

____

3. Erin did not have plans. She could visit Dora.

____

____

4. Erin could bring a game. She could bring a movie.

____

____

Name ______________________ Date ____________

Spelling Word Sort

Write each Basic Word under the correct heading.

Long *a* Spelled *ay*	Long *a* Spelled *ai*
______	______
______	______
______	______
______	______
______	______

Long *e* Spelled *ee*	Long *e* Spelled *ea*
______	______
______	______
______	______
______	______
______	______
______	______

Spelling Words

Basic

1. lay
2. real
3. trail
4. sweet
5. today
6. dream
7. seem
8. tea
9. treat
10. afraid
11. leave
12. bait
13. cheer
14. speed

Review

paint
please

Challenge

yesterday
explain

Review: Add the Review Words to your Word Sort.

Challenge: Add the Challenge Words to your Word Sort.

Name ______________________ Date ____________

Focus Trait: Voice

Express Thoughts and Feelings

These thoughts and feelings...	...help you understand this.
Destiny remembers how much she enjoyed talking with writers. She describes how they shared her love of words.	They show how Destiny feels about talking to authors, and they explain why Destiny wants to become a writer.

A. Read the event from *Destiny's Gift*. Underline the words that show Destiny's thoughts and feelings. Then explain what they help you understand about Destiny.

These thoughts and feelings...	...help you understand this.
1. Destiny can't stop crying after she finds out about Mrs. Wade's store.	

B. Read each sentence that tells an event from *Destiny's Gift*. Look at the page listed. Write a sentence that tells about Destiny's or Mrs. Wade's thoughts and feelings.

Pair/Share **Work with a partner before you write.**

Event	Sentence with Thoughts and Feelings
2. Page 88: Destiny says she likes Mrs. Wade's bookstore.	
3. Page 104: Destiny writes something for Mrs. Wade.	

Name ______________________ Date ____________

Cumulative Review

Read the grocery list. Write each item in the chart below.

Grocery List

artichokes	grapes	peaches
beans	lemonade	peanuts
beef	limes	pineapple
cheese	grains	prunes
coffee	oatmeal	crayfish

Long a		Long e		Long i spelled VC*e*	Long o spelled VC*e*	Long u spelled VC*e*
VC*e*		VC*e*				
ai		ee				
ay		ea				

Write a recipe on another sheet of paper. Use at least three words on the list. You can use other ingredients, too.

Destiny's Gift

What's the Word?

You see the big, thick dictionary Mrs. Wade keeps on a pedestal in her bookstore. You flip open the dictionary and see the word *content*. You read:

content *adjective:* satisfied with what one is or has

Read page 92. How does the word *content* help describe Destiny and Mrs. Wade?

____

____

Next, you flip the dictionary to another page and see the word *worried*. You read:

worried *adjective:* concerned, filled with worry

Read page 96. How does the word *worried* help describe Mrs. Wade?

____

____

Finally, you flip through the dictionary to another page and see the word *inspired*. You read:

inspired *adjective:* filled with the spirit to do something

Read page 104. How does the word *inspired* help describe Destiny?

____

____

Name ______________________ Date ______

Destiny has used many interesting words in her notebook called "Mrs. Wade's Bookstore."

Read pages 104–107. Finish writing this page in Destiny's notebook. Tell how she feels about what is happening to the store. Use the dictionary words and any other words you might need.

Mrs. Wade's bookstore might close! There are so many reasons I love that bookstore and so many reasons I will be sad if it closes.

Name ______________________ Date ____________

Run-On Sentences

- Two or more simple sentences that run together are called **run-on** sentences.
- A run-on sentence may be corrected by forming a **compound sentence**. The conjunctions *and*, *but*, *or*, and *so* are used to form compound sentences.

  Rita does not like moose Gwen does.
  Rita does not like moose, but Gwen does.

Thinking Question
Can I use a conjunction to join these sentences and form a compound sentence?

Correct each run-on sentence by forming a compound sentence. Write the conjunction and then write the compound sentence.

1. Moose are a kind of deer they are part of the deer family.

____

____

2. Adult males have large antlers female moose do not.

____

____

3. Moose are good swimmers they are fast runners.

____

____

4. The moose might bellow the moose might grunt.

____

____

Name ______________________ Date ____________

Long *a* and Long *e* Spellings

Write a Basic Word to answer each clue. Then use letters in the word to answer the second clue. The letters may not be in the correct order.

Spelling Words

Basic

1. lay
2. real
3. trail
4. sweet
5. today
6. dream
7. seem
8. tea
9. treat
10. afraid
11. leave
12. bait
13. screen
14. speed

Review

paint
please

Challenge

yesterday
explain

1. what helps you catch fish ___ ___ ___ ___

what you swing in baseball ___ ___ ___

2. how fast you go ___ ___ ___ ___ ___

not shallow ___ ___ ___ ___

3. something you do when you sleep ___ ___ ___ ___ ___

what you do with a book ___ ___ ___ ___

4. candy has this taste ___ ___ ___ ___ ___

a direction on a map ___ ___ ___ ___

5. a reward for a good dog ___ ___ ___ ___ ___

what you do with food ___ ___ ___

6. to go away ___ ___ ___ ___ ___

a snake-like fish ___ ___ ___

7. to look or appear to be true ___ ___ ___ ___

your eyes do this for you ___ ___ ___

8. something you might walk on in the woods ___ ___ ___ ___ ___

a rodent with a long tail ___ ___ ___

Name ______________________ Date ____________

Antonyms

lower	all	left
after	take	last

Read each word below. Write the antonym from the box above. Then write a sentence using both words.

1. none ______________

____

2. first ______________

____

3. raise ______________

____

4. right ______________

____

5. before ______________

____

6. give ______________

____

Name _______________________ Date ____________

Kinds of Sentences

- There are four kinds of sentences.

Mom is home.	**Declarative** (statement)
Did you study?	**Interrogative** (question)
Pick up that mess.	**Imperative** (command)
What a great job!	**Exclamatory** (exclamation)

Write *statement* if the sentence tells something. Write *question* if the sentence asks something.

1. John brought his lunch to the picnic. ________________

2. Are you going to the picnic? ________________

3. Will you bring a friend? ________________

Write *command* if the sentence tells someone to do something. Write *exclamation* if the sentence shows strong feeling.

4. The picnic is really going to be fun! ________________

5. Hand me that plate. ________________

6. Wait for me over there. ________________

Name ______________________ Date __________

Proofreading for Spelling

Read each sign. Find and circle the misspelled words.

1. Plees do not feed the bears.

2. Spead Limit 55 Miles per Hour

3. Stay on the traiyl.

4. Sweete tee $1.00
Peanuts $.50

5. The zoo will close todaiy at 4 PM.

6. Leeve your shoes outside.

7. Stay out! Wet paynt.

8. Do not be afrad to try new things.

Write the misspelled words correctly on the lines below.

1. ______________
2. ______________
3. ______________
4. ______________
5. ______________
6. ______________
7. ______________
8. ______________

Spelling Words

Basic

1. lay
2. real
3. trail
4. sweet
5. today
6. dream
7. seem
8. tea
9. treat
10. afraid
11. leave
12. bait
13. screen
14. speed

Review

paint
please

Challenge

yesterday
explain

Name ______________________ Date ____________

Connect to Writing

Too many short sentences make writing sound choppy. Sometimes you can combine two short sentences to make one longer compound sentence. Use a comma (,) and the conjunction *and, but,* or *or* to form compound sentences.

Short Sentences	Compound Sentence
Libby owns many books. She hasn't read them all.	Libby owns many books, but she hasn't read them all.

Use a conjunction to form compound sentences.

1. Victoria came to our book party. She brought ten books.

____

____

2. We could hike on Saturday. We could wait until Sunday.

____

____

Correct these run-ons by using a conjunction to form compound sentences.

3. People could bring books they could bring magazines.

____

____

4. These books are very interesting they are hard to understand.

____

____

Name ______________________ Date ____________

Long *o* Spelled *oa*, *ow*

Each word in the Word Bank is in the puzzle. Find and circle each word in the puzzle. Words can be across or down.

arrow	floating	undertow
below	goal	upload
blown	slow	
coach	throwing	

p	u	p	l	o	a	d	n	u	p
o	b	l	o	p	r	r	f	n	b
b	l	o	w	n	e	u	l	d	e
e	o	t	h	r	t	h	o	e	c
l	c	o	a	c	h	s	a	r	o
o	g	w	r	a	r	l	t	t	h
w	o	i	b	b	r	o	i	o	b
n	a	a	r	r	o	w	n	w	o
l	l	p	e	n	i	n	g	b	a
g	t	h	r	o	w	i	n	g	c

On a separate sheet of paper, use each word in the Word Bank in a sentence. Read your sentences aloud.

Name ____________________ Date __________

Identifying Nouns and Subjects

- A word that names a person, a place, or a thing is a **noun**. The noun that is doing something in a sentence is the subject.

  My mom helped to build the new road.

  The work lasted one year.

Thinking Questions
Is the word naming a person, a place, or a thing? Which noun tells who or what is doing something?

Write the two nouns in each sentence. Circle the subject of each sentence.

1. Workers brought in tables. ____________________
2. High winds knocked down the tents. ____________________
3. The sand blew into the food. ____________________
4. The moon was beautiful at night. ____________________
5. My family did some work. ____________________
6. My cousin showed the workers where to go.
   ____
7. My brother played some music. ____________________
8. My uncle put up the signs. ____________________
9. Her mother brought food sometimes. ____________________
10. The mayor visited when the road was done.
    ____

Name ______________________ Date ____________

Pop's Bridge
Grammar:
Common and Proper Nouns

Capitalizing Nouns

- A word that names a person, place, or thing is a noun.
- **Common nouns** name any person, place, or thing. **Proper nouns** name a particular person, place, or thing.
- Proper nouns begin with capital letters and may have more than one word. People's titles and important words in titles of books are capitalized.

  His daughter Audrey visited him at his job in England.

Thinking Question
Does the noun name any person, place, or thing, or does it name a particular person, place, or thing?

Write *common* or *proper* for each underlined noun.

1. Outside of Atlanta, Jessie's father works in an office. ______________
2. Bennie came to his father's bicycle shop. ______________
3. Many parents invite their children to the places they work. ______________
4. Mike went to New York City with his mother. ______________
5. They saw a parade and ate great food. ______________
6. Gary's father took him to an Ice Age display at the museum. ______________

Name ______________________ Date ______________

Spelling Word Sort

Write each Basic Word under the correct heading.

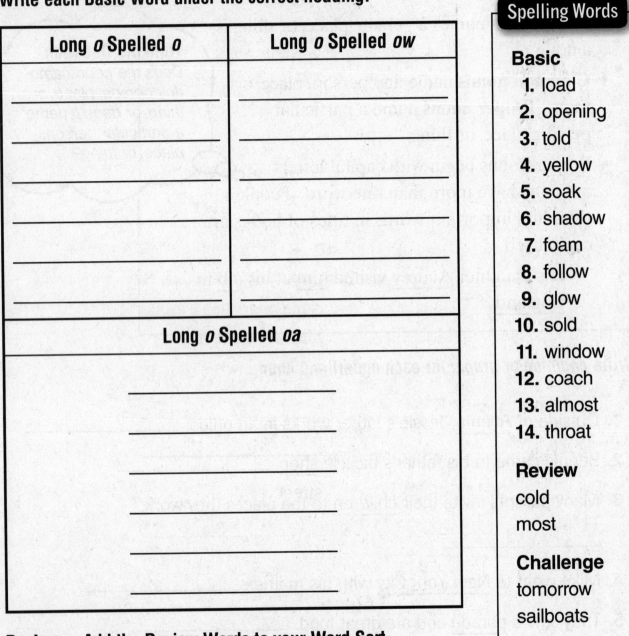

Long *o* Spelled *o*	Long *o* Spelled *ow*

Long *o* Spelled *oa*

Spelling Words

Basic

1. load
2. opening
3. told
4. yellow
5. soak
6. shadow
7. foam
8. follow
9. glow
10. sold
11. window
12. coach
13. almost
14. throat

Review

cold
most

Challenge

tomorrow
sailboats

Review: Add the Review Words to your Word Sort.

Challenge: Add the Challenge Words to your Word Sort.

Name ______________________ Date ____________

Pop's Bridge
Writing:
Narrative Writing

Focus Trait: Ideas

Important and Interesting Details

Good writers use interesting details to help readers understand their ideas.

For example:

The girl rode her bike.

The above sentence would be much more interesting with important details added:

The small redheaded girl proudly rode her shiny new yellow bike to school.

Read each sentence and look at the illustration from "Pop's Bridge" on the page listed. Add interesting details to each sentence.

1. Page 134: The family looked at the bridge.

____

____

2. Page 137: The boy shouted on the street.

____

____

3. Page 143: Robert was happy.

____

____

4. Page 144: He cut the puzzle piece.

____

____

Name ______________________ Date ____________

Cumulative Review

Read each clue. Unscramble the letters and write the word that answers the clue. Read the words you made.

1. This is a food. Many people eat it in the morning. mtoeala ____________
2. You might do this if you do not want to do something. anlcopmi ____________
3. Cars drive fast on these kinds of roads. They have two or more lanes. whgysiha ____________
4. This is a way to heat bread. tasot ____________
5. This can take you across the sea, when it's windy. alitabos ____________
6. This number is the answer to these math problems: 5 X 3 and 5 + 5 + 5. efnietf ____________
7. There are four of these. They are winter, spring, summer, and fall. eosnsas ____________
8. This is the color of a lemon. lelwyo ____________
9. This describes something that never moves very quickly. wols ____________
10. This can help you find your way when you are driving. pdraaom ____________

Pop's Bridge

More Views from the Bridge

Mr. Shu, Charlie's dad, is writing a letter to his family in China about what it is like to work on the Golden Gate Bridge. Use the text and illustrations to help you write the letter.

Read page 130. What was it like to be a painter on the Golden Gate Bridge?

Dear Family,

I am working as a painter on the Golden Gate Bridge! You would not believe how big it is! Guess what I do? Every morning I

It is hard work to be a painter because

Sometimes I am afraid that

I really like being a painter on the bridge. It is exciting work. I will tell you more when the bridge is finally done.

Love to everyone,

Chang Shu

Name ______________________________ Date ______

Charlie Shu has just been to the party at Robert's house to celebrate the opening day of the bridge. He is writing a journal entry about it.

Read pages 144–147. What was the party like for Charlie?

Today was opening day at the bridge! It was so thrilling. After we walked across the bridge, there was a big party at Robert's house.

There were a lot of people and food at the party. I felt ______________________________

____

Remember that puzzle we were doing? Robert had the missing piece all along! My dad and Robert's dad put the piece in together. This made me feel

____

____

For awhile I thought Robert believed his dad was better than mine. But now I know that

____

____

It was a really good day for a lot of reasons!

Name ______________________ Date __________

Common and Proper Nouns

Write the two nouns in each sentence. Circle the noun that is the subject of the sentence.

1. The boys watched the hotel being taken down. ______________
2. A large ball knocked down the old walls. ______________
3. A new building would go up in that space. ______________
4. Soon, a huge hole was in the ground. ______________

Write *common* or *proper* for each underlined noun.

5. We learned about the Rocky Mountains in school. ______________
6. My aunt came all the way from Canada. ______________
7. The crowd rode horses. ______________
8. It was an exciting day. ______________

Write the sentences correctly. Capitalize the appropriate underlined words.

9. We went with mrs. benitez to the museum of natural history.

____

10. We bought a book called animals in the wild.

____

Name ______________________ Date ____________

Long *o* Spellings

In the spaces below, write a Spelling Word to complete each newspaper ad.

1. The Shoe Store is ________! Come in and try on a pair of our great shoes.

2. ________ Washers We'll clean your glass!

3. Enjoy the ________ of a warm fire! Buy a ________ of our firewood.

4. Do you like baseball? Baseball ________ needed to work with children. Apply in person.

5. Garage Sale today and ________. ________ the signs to our house.

6. Store Closing Sale We cannot close until everything is ________.

Spelling Words

Basic

1. load
2. open
3. told
4. yellow
5. soak
6. shadow
7. foam
8. follow
9. glow
10. sold
11. window
12. coach
13. almost
14. throat

Review

cold
most

Challenge

tomorrow
sailboats

1. ________________
2. ________________
3. ________________, ________________
4. ________________
5. ________________, ________________
6. ________________

Name ______________________ Date ____________

Word Families

Read each sentence. Use your understanding of the base word to figure out the meaning of the underlined word. Write the base word and the meaning of the underlined word.

1. The window display did not look good, so the crew had to rethink where to put the items.

   ____

2. The children were clinging to each other because of the cold wind.

   ____

3. The excitement over the team's win caused a celebration that lasted hours.

   ____

4. They stretched the rope across the yard.

   ____

5. As the day became foggier, it became impossible to see the mountains.

   ____

6. The player was balancing the basketball on one finger, spinning it faster and faster.

   ____

7. After another sock disappears, Dad buys a new package of socks.

   ____

8. It was unbelievable how close the water came during the high tide.

   ____

Name ____________________ Date ____________

Pop's Bridge
Grammar:
Spiral Review

Compound Sentences

- A **compound sentence** is made up of two **simple sentences** joined by a comma followed by a **conjunction**.
- The words *and*, *but*, *or*, and *so* are conjunctions.
- Two simple sentences that run together without using a comma and a conjunction are called a **run-on** sentence.

Simple sentences: Nina will go to the concert. She will go to the movies.

Run-on sentence: Nina will go to the concert she will go to the movies.

Compound sentence: Nina will go to the concert, or she will go to the movies.

Write the conjunction that best joins the two simple sentences into one compound sentence. Then write the compound sentence.

1. Roy wears his helmet. He wears his kneepads.

____

2. Betsy will use her gloves. She will borrow a pair.

____

Correct the run-on sentence by using a comma and a conjunction to form a compound sentence.

3. Riding is fun I like hiking better.

____

4. We can ride today we can hike tomorrow.

____

Name ____________________ Date __________

Proofreading for Spelling

Pop's Bridge
Spelling:
Long *o* Spellings

Read the following newspaper article. Find and circle the misspelled words.

Yelloaw Jackets Win First Game

The stadium was owpen for the game. Coch Smith and her players were ready. The game was sould out. Not even the coald weather kept people away. The crowd cheered as the team entered the stadium.

The first batter scored a run almowst right away. During the game, nine more players folloawed her lead. The Yellow Jackets left the other team in the shados.

A player towld me after the game that they intend to win every game this season. They will be put to the test tomorroaw when they play the Colts.

Spelling Words

Basic

1. load
2. open
3. told
4. yellow
5. soak
6. shadow
7. foam
8. follow
9. glow
10. sold
11. window
12. coach
13. almost
14. throat

Review

cold
most

Challenge

tomorrow
sailboats

Write the misspelled words correctly on the lines below.

1. ____________ 6. ____________
2. ____________ 7. ____________
3. ____________ 8. ____________
4. ____________ 9. ____________
5. ____________ 10. ____________

Name ______________________ Date ____________

Connect to Writing

Using exact nouns helps make your writing clearer and more interesting.

Less-Exact Noun	More-Exact Noun
road	superhighway
area	valley

Replace each underlined noun in the sentences with a more exact noun. Use the nouns in the word box.

ranch	coyotes	ponies
thunderstorms	city	cowboys

1. Ernie saw two men through his binoculars. ____________
2. They were rounding up some animals. ____________
3. Off to one side, some wild animals were hard to see. ____________
4. Faraway, the sky was filled with rain. ____________
5. They worked hard to get people back to their home. ____________

Correctly capitalize the proper noun, personal title, and book title.

6. (proper noun) new mexico ____________
7. (personal title) mrs. lopez ____________
8. (book title) amazing bridges from around the world

____

Name ______________________ Date ____________

Roberto Clemente

Phonics:
Long *i* Spelled *i, ie, igh*

Long *i* Spelled *i*, *ie*, *igh*

Read each sentence. Choose the missing word from the box. Write the word in the blank.

find	climb	fried
sights	wild	lie
sigh	untied	
tried	midnight	

1. I did not ______________ the book I was looking for.
2. The clock strikes twelve at ______________.
3. Jasmine and her family went into the city to see the ______________.
4. The ______________ animal ran through the forest.
5. I would like to ______________ a mountain some day.
6. I tripped over my shoelaces because they were ______________.
7. The best dish at this restaurant is ______________ chicken.
8. "I wish it would stop raining," Marty said with a ______________.
9. The police officer ______________ to direct traffic.
10. George Washington once said, "I cannot tell a ______________."

Name ______________________ Date ____________

Identifying Singular and Plural Nouns

- A noun that names only one person, place, or thing is a **singular noun**. A noun that names more than one person, place, or thing is a **plural noun**.
- Add *-s* to most singular nouns to form the plural.

  The children played a ball game.
  The children played ball games.
  They ran from place to place.
  They ran to different places.

Thinking Question
Is the word naming only one person, place, or thing or is the word naming more than one person, place, or thing?

Write *singular* or *plural* for each underlined noun.

1. Many kids played ball games long ago. ______________
2. The ball was made of cloth. ______________
3. One player ran between two stones. ______________
4. They would throw the ball at a runner. ______________

Write the plural form of the noun in parentheses to complete the sentence.

5. Later, teams drew ______________ on the field. (line)
6. Teams built ______________ for another edge of the field. (wall)
7. Some ______________ would throw the ball underhand. (pitcher)
8. Some games would last twelve ______________. (hour)

Name ______________________ Date ____________

Plural Nouns with *-s*

Roberto Clemente

Grammar:
Plural Nouns with *-s* and *-es*

- Add *-s* to most nouns to form the plural.

Singular:	*team*	*cap*	*bat*
Plural:	*teams*	*caps*	*bats*

Thinking Question
Do I add -s to form the plural?

Write the plural form of the underlined noun.

1. They put a new stain on the floor.

   They tested two different ______________ to see which would be darker.

2. Portia slipped and fell with a loud bang.

   A few minutes later, there were two louder ______________.

3. The basketball player wore high-top sneakers.

   More ______________ started wearing them after the first game.

4. The light came on when he fell into the switch.

   After three people fell, more ______________ came on.

5. They put a sign on the ground to warn people not to slip.

   At the end of the day, there were a dozen ______________ in that area.

Name ______________________ Date ____________

Roberto Clemente

Spelling:
Long *i* Spellings

Spelling Word Sort

Write each Basic Word under the correct heading.

Long *i* Spelled *i*	Long *i* Spelled *ie*
______	______
______	______
______	______
______	______
______	______

Long *i* Spelled *igh*	
______	______
______	______
______	______
______	______

Review: Add the Review Words to your Word Sort.

Challenge: What letter or letters form the long *i* sound in the two Challenge Words?

______________________; ______________________

Spelling Words

Basic

1. slight
2. mild
3. sight
4. pie
5. mind
6. tie
7. pilot
8. might
9. lie
10. tight
11. blind
12. fight
13. dies
14. midnight

Review

find
night

Challenge

silent
frightening

Name ______________________ Date ____________

Roberto Clemente

Writing:
Narrative Writing

Focus Trait: Sentence Fluency

Time-Order Words

Writers use transition words, or time-order words, to show when events happen. For example:

After they won the championship game, all the boys on Pedro's soccer team cheered and high-fived each other. Next, they went out for pizza to celebrate.

Read the following paragraph. In each blank, fill in the phrase from the box that fits best.

Then	Yesterday morning
Afterwards	During the game
Before I left the house	When I got to the field

1. ________________, I woke up with butterflies in my stomach. It was the day of my first softball game! Immediately, I jumped out of bed. **2.** ____________ I put on my new uniform and ran downstairs for breakfast. **3.** ________________, I reminded my mother to take the camera to the game. **4.** ____________________, my teammates were there practicing. **5.** ________________, I got two hits and one run! In the end, we won the game by one point. **6.** ________________, my mother took me out for ice cream.

Name ______________________ Date ____________

Cumulative Review

Write a word from the box to complete each sentence.

most	lightning	flowed
slimy	toast	railroad
tries	knights	
glowing	title	

1. Lava ______________ down the sides of the volcano and into the sea.
2. A bolt of ______________ suddenly flashed across the sky.
3. What is the ______________ of your favorite book?
4. For breakfast, Karl likes to eat ______________ with peanut butter.
5. I love to watch the fireflies ______________ in the dark summer sky.
6. King Arthur and his ______________ sat at a huge round table.
7. The worm felt ______________ when I touched it.
8. Always stop, look, and listen before crossing a ______________ track.
9. The athlete finally jumped over the bar after three ______________.
10. Lee knew ______________ of the answers on the test, but not all of them.

Roberto Clemente

1960 World Series Program

The Pittsburgh Pirates are going to play the New York Yankees. Use examples from the text to fill out each section of the program for famous hitter Roberto Clemente.

Read page 170. Use the information on this page to tell how Clemente started out playing baseball.

1960 World Series
Pittsburgh Pirate Roberto Clemente

How Roberto Clemente Got Started

____

____

____

Read page 172. Use what you read to write about how Clemente ended up in Pittsburgh. What was it like for him?

Why Roberto Clemente Came to Pittsburgh

____

____

____

Name ______________________ Date ______

Roberto Clemente
Independent Reading

Read pages 173–174. Why was Clemente's first game with the Pirates so important?

Roberto Clemente's First Game with the Pirates

____

____

____

Read pages 175–176. Why did so many children love Roberto Clemente?

Roberto Clemente Has Many Fans

____

____

____

Read page 177. How do you think Roberto Clemente felt right before the World Series? Why do you think he felt that way? Imagine you are Roberto Clemente and tell fans how you feel about playing in the World Series.

Roberto Clemente in His Own Words

____

____

____

____

____

Name ______________________ Date __________

Plural Nouns with *-s* and *-es*

Write *singular* or *plural* for each underlined noun.

1. The fans went to find their <u>seats</u>. ______________
2. The popcorn seller brought them two <u>boxes</u>. ______________
3. Other fans passed a giant <u>ball</u> around. ______________
4. A foul ball sailed up into the stands from the <u>field</u>. ______________
5. Some fans had special <u>passes</u> that let them go onto the field. ______________

Write the plural form of the noun in parentheses to complete the sentence.

6. Two ______________ had wire mesh that stopped foul balls. (fence)
7. People stood in the ______________ instead of sitting in their seats. (aisle)
8. The fans clapped for a series of great ______________ of hard-hit balls. (catch)
9. The scoreboard could not show any ______________, because that number was broken. (six)
10. There were ______________ of programs to hand out to the fans. (stack)

Name ______________________ Date ____________

Long *i* Spellings

Write a Basic Word to answer each question.

1. If you were eating a round dessert with a flaky crust, what would you be eating? ______________

2. What is the opposite of loose? ______________

3. What is the time when one day ends and another begins? ______________

4. What would a man wear around his neck if he was getting dressed up? ______________

5. If you did not tell the truth, what did you tell? ______________

6. Who flies a plane? ______________

7. What do you think with? ______________

8. What does a boxer have to do? ______________

Spelling Words

Basic

1. slight
2. mild
3. sight
4. pie
5. mind
6. tie
7. pilot
8. might
9. lie
10. tight
11. blind
12. fight
13. die
14. midnight

Review

find
night

Challenge

silent
frightening

Prefix *mis-*

Read the letter. Notice the underlined words. Write a reply to this letter. Use at least four of the underlined words in your letter.

Dear Friend,

I did not mean to misbehave or to mistreat you. I thought it was funny when someone mispronounced your name. I didn't think it would upset you, but I can see that I miscalculated that. If someone said I did not want to be your friend, then they are misinformed. Can we please forget about this misunderstanding?

Your friend

____

____

____

____

____

____

____

____

____

____

____

Name ______________________ Date ____________

Commas in Sentences

- **Commas** are used in a date or when listing city and state in a sentence.
- Commas are also used when combining sentences and when using nouns or verbs in a series.

  On June 3, 1973, in Chicago, Illinois, they played baseball, football, and soccer.

Rewrite each sentence with a comma where it belongs in a date or a place.

1. They loaded the plane bringing supplies on December 29 1972.

____

2. It was headed for Managua Nicaragua.

____

Combine each group of sentences. Put the nouns or verbs in a series with commas. Write the new sentence.

3. The plane carried food. The plane carried water.
The plane carried supplies.

____

4. A pilot was onboard. A baseball star was onboard.
A helper was onboard.

____

Name ______________________ Date ____________

Roberto Clemente

Spelling:
Long *i* Spellings

Proofreading for Spelling

Find the misspelled words and circle them.

Plane Has Narrow Escape

A brave pielot saved the lives of her passengers yesterday when she saved an airplane from crashing.

Captain Jo Ann Foster was flying at 35,000 feet at midnite when her plane began to rock. There was only a sliet wind, so she knew her plane was in trouble. An engine was out, and the plane was sinking. Not only that, but thick fog made her have to fly blighnd. She was in a tite spot.

Captain Foster quickly thought of things she mite do. Different ideas went through her miend. She would have to fite to guide her plane to safety.

"I felt some miled fear," she said later, "but I was mainly thinking of how to save the plane and the passengers."

She found the nearest airport on the map and steered toward it. Finally, the airport came in siet. Captain Foster made a perfect landing, and 147 passengers were safe.

Spelling Words

Basic

1. slight
2. mild
3. sight
4. pie
5. mind
6. tie
7. pilot
8. might
9. lie
10. tight
11. blind
12. fight
13. die
14. midnight

Review

find
night

Challenge

silent
frightening

Write the misspelled words correctly on the lines below.

1. ______________ 6. ______________

2. ______________ 7. ______________

3. ______________ 8. ______________

4. ______________ 9. ______________

5. ______________ 10. ______________

Name ____________________ Date ____________

Connect to Writing

Using the correct spelling of plural nouns makes your writing clearer and easier to understand. Add *-s* to form the plural of most singular nouns. Add *-es* to form the plural of a singular noun that ends with *s, sh, ch,* or *x*.

Sentences With Singular Nouns That Should be Plural Nouns	Sentences with Correct Plural Nouns
The baseball player tried two bat before choosing one.	The baseball player tried two bats before choosing one.
The teams sat on two bench.	The team sat on two benches.

Circle the singular noun that should be plural in each sentence. Then write the sentence using the plural spelling of the noun.

1. The fans rode to the baseball game in ten bus.

____

2. Most of the fans have already been to a few game this year.

____

3. Juan and Mary took their baseball glove to the game.

____

4. The pitcher made two great catch.

____

5. Another player made two good toss to first base.

____

Name ______________________ Date __________

Bat Loves the Night
Phonics: Words with the VCV Pattern

VCV Words with Long and Short Vowels

Read each sentence. Choose the missing word from the box. Write the word. Then reread the complete sentence.

visit	robot	flavor
tiny	limit	shiver
report	decide	gravel

1. We took a bumpy ride down a ______________ road in the country.
2. Chocolate is my favorite ______________ of ice cream.
3. I ______________ the amount of sweets that I eat.
4. My sister has a collection of ______________ glass animals.
5. I need to pick a topic for my ______________.
6. It was hard to ______________ which movie to watch.
7. The icy rain made me ______________.
8. Steve hopes to ______________ the Space Museum someday.
9. That interesting machine is called a ______________.

Name ______________________ Date ____________

Action Verbs

A word that tells what people or things do is a **verb**. Words that show action, or something that is done, are **action verbs**.

The owl **blinked** its eyes.

It **slept** in a hollow tree.

Thinking Question
What is the subject doing?

Each sentence has one action verb. Write the action verb on the line.

1. Some animals sleep during the day. ______________
2. They look for food at night. ______________
3. Owls see well in the dark. ______________
4. The owl spread its wings wide. ______________
5. Then it flew from the tree. ______________
6. It beat its wings quietly. ______________
7. The owl spotted a small mouse. ______________
8. It swooped down for the mouse. ______________
9. The mouse hid in a hollow log. ______________
10. The owl returned to its tree. ______________

Being Verbs

Bat Loves the Night
Grammar:
What Is a Verb?

Some verbs do not show action. The verbs *am*, *is*, *are*, *was*, and *were* are examples of **being verbs.** They are forms of the verb *be*. They tell what someone or something is or was.

I ***am*** interested in bats.
I ***was*** proud of my knowledge of bats.
They ***are*** amazing flyers.
You ***were*** last at the zoo.
He ***is*** skilled at identifying bats.
We ***were*** excited at the zoo.

Am, *is*, and *are* show present tense. *Was* and *were* show past tense.

Thinking Question
What does the sentence tell me about what the subject is or was?

Write the being verb on the line. Write *present* or *past* for each verb.

1. My father was nice to my class. ______________
2. He is kind and gives us his zoo passes. ______________
3. We were thankful. ______________
4. The boys are upset when they cannot go. ______________
5. You are good to help us. ______________
6. Most people are happy with the idea. ______________
7. They were surprised when we asked. ______________
8. They are annoyed sometimes but not often. ______________
9. I am careful to ask nicely. ______________
10. I was friendly to everyone. ______________

Name ____________________ Date __________

Bat Loves the Night
Spelling:
More Short and Long Vowels

Spelling Word Sort

Write each Basic Word in the box where it belongs. You will write words with two vowel sounds in more than one box.

Vowel sound in *rope*	Vowel sound in *meet*
____________	____________
____________	____________
____________	____________
____________	____________
Vowel sound in *came*	**Vowel sound in *bite***
____________	____________
____________	____________
____________	____________
Vowel sound in *blue*	**Vowel sound in *flat***
____________	____________
____________	____________
Vowel sound in *cup*	**Vowel sound in *dress***
____________	____________
Vowel sound in *skip*	**Vowel sound in *odd***
____________	____________
____________	____________

Spelling Words

Basic

1. math
2. toast
3. easy
4. socks
5. Friday
6. stuff
7. paid
8. cheese
9. June
10. elbow
11. program
12. shiny
13. piles
14. sticky

Review

each
both

Challenge

comb
holiday

Challenge: Add the Challenge Words to your Word Sort.

Name ______________________ Date ____________

Focus Trait: Ideas

Details and Examples

Writer's Idea	Details and Examples
Bats hang upside down.	Bats' toes are shaped like hooks, so it's no effort for a bat to hang upside down.

A. Read each of the writer's ideas. Find the details and examples from *Bat Loves the Night* that help explain the idea. Complete the sentences.

Writer's Idea	Details and Examples
1. Bats use their wings like we use our arms and hands.	A bat's wing is its __________ and hand. Four __________ fingers __________ the skin of the wing.
2. Bats use sound to locate things in the dark.	She __________ her voice around her like a __________ , and the echoes come singing back. They carry a sound __________ of all her voice has touched.

B. Read the writer's idea. Look at the pages from *Bat Loves the Night*. Write details and examples that help explain the idea.

Pair/Share **Work with a partner to find sentences in the story that include details and examples that support the writer's idea.**

Writer's Idea	Details and Examples
3. Baby bats mature quickly.	

Name ______________________ Date ____________

Cumulative Review

Write a word from the box to complete each sentence. Then read the complete sentence.

pilot	planet	tiger
second	visit	bacon
flavor	finish	cabins

1. Can we play outside after we ________________ our homework?
2. My cousins came to ________________ us last summer.
3. As we were leaving the plane, the ________________ shook my hand.
4. The scouts stayed in small ________________ near the lake.
5. Chocolate is the ________________ of ice cream that I like best.
6. Would you like ________________ with your eggs?
7. Look! That reddish light in the sky is the ________________ Mars!
8. Brad came in ________________ in the race, right behind Jay.
9. We watched a ________________ sleep under the tree.

Name ______________________________ Date ______

Bat Loves the Night

File a Missing Bat Report

One night you were looking out of your window with your binoculars when you saw a bat flying through the sky. Scientists who are tracking the bat want some information, and you have that information. Fill out this missing bat report using information from the text.

Read pages 212–214. What was the first thing you saw the bat do when you looked out the window?

____

____

Read pages 215–217. Someone reported the bat was swooping and gliding through the sky. What do you think she was doing?

____

____

Read pages 218–219. We have evidence that a moth showed up at some point. Did you see what happened? Tell us, step by step.

First, ____________________________________

Then, ____________________________________

Finally, __________________________________

Name ______________________________ Date ______

Bat Loves the Night
Independent Reading

Read pages 220–221. You are the only one to see where the bat went next. Describe what happened.

____

____

Read pages 222–224. We suspect that there are baby bats living in the barn. Tell us everything you know about the babies.

____

____

Read page 225. Now we think we know where the bat is. What do you think the bat is doing? When can we see this bat again?

____

____

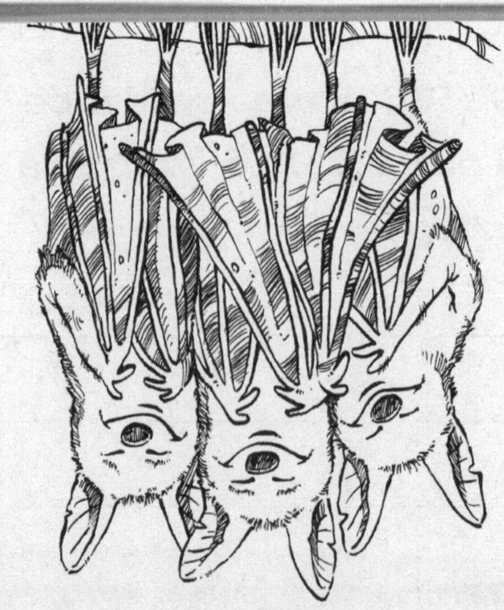

Name ______________________ Date ____________

Action Verbs and Being Verbs

There is one action verb in each sentence. Write the verb on the line.

1. Randy looked for a book about bats. ______________
2. He found one in the back shelf. ______________
3. He searched for new facts. ______________
4. He learned that bats do not live in Antarctica. ______________
5. He borrowed the book. ______________

Write the being verb on the line. Then write *present* or *past*.

6. We are walking on a nature trail. ______________
7. You were thoughtful to bring the binoculars. ______________
8. I am able to see through the binoculars. ______________
9. We are tired of walking in the heat. ______________
10. The guides were searching for hidden caves. ______________

Name ______________________ Date ____________

More Short and Long Vowels

Write the Basic Words that match each heading.

Spelling Words

Basic
1. math
2. toast
3. easy
4. socks
5. Friday
6. stuff
7. paid
8. cheese
9. June
10. elbow
11. program
12. shiny
13. piles
14. sticky

Review
each
both

Challenge
comb
holiday

Proper Nouns

1. ____________
2. ____________

Common Nouns

3. ____________
4. ____________
5. ____________
6. ____________
7. ____________
8. ____________
9. ____________
10. ____________

Describing Words

11. ____________
12. ____________
13. ____________

Verb

14. ____________

On the line below, write a sentence using one word from each group above.

15. ____

____

Name ______________________ Date __________

Suffixes *-able, -ible*

Write a sentence using the words provided. Make sure the sentence helps the reader understand the meaning of the word.

1. agreeable

____

2. valuable

____

3. reversible

____

4. comfortable

____

5. breakable

____

6. sensible

____

7. spreadable

____

8. flexible

____

Name ______________________ Date ______________

Complete Subjects and Predicates

- A sentence is a group of words that tells a complete thought and has a complete subject and a complete predicate.
- The **subject** tells whom or what the sentence is about and usually comes at the beginning of the sentence.
- The **predicate** tells what the subject does or is, and it can be one word or more than one word.

Many different words	tell about the same idea.
Subject	**Predicate**

Write the subject or the predicate of each sentence.

1. Tommy cut pictures from the magazine. (subject) ______________
2. He and his friends glued them to a poster. (predicate)

____

Combine each pair of sentences. Use a conjunction to form a compound subject in each new sentence. Write the new sentence on the line.

3. My friends gathered magazines about animals. The teachers gathered magazines about animals.

____

4. The kids carried the magazines. The teachers carried the magazines.

____

Name ______________________ Date ____________

Proofreading for Spelling

Bat Loves the Night
Spelling:
More Short and Long Vowels

Find the misspelled words and circle them.

Jun 1: This was a great day! It started out like any other Frieday. I did all the usual stufe. I got dressed, put on my shoes and soks, and ate some tost and jam. But as I started to coamb my hair, I heard kids playing outside. For a minute, I thought it might be a holliday. Then suddenly I remembered that school is out. This is the first day of summer vacation! There are no more mathe tests, no more pils of homework, and no more long days of sitting still.

The rest of the day was perfect. I played kickball with my friends, rode my bike, and went to the pool. It was so much fun that I think I'll do it all again tomorrow. Or maybe I'll just read a book and take it eazy. I love summer!

Spelling Words

Basic

1. math
2. toast
3. easy
4. socks
5. Friday
6. stuff
7. paid
8. cheese
9. June
10. elbow
11. program
12. shiny
13. piles
14. sticky

Review

each
both

Challenge

comb
holiday

Write the misspelled words correctly on the lines below.

1. ____________ 6. ____________

2. ____________ 7. ____________

3. ____________ 8. ____________

4. ____________ 9. ____________

5. ____________ 10. ____________

Name _________________________ Date ___________

Connect to Writing

If the subject you are writing about is doing more than one action, you can tell about it in one sentence. You can combine more than one simple predicate to form a compound predicate. This can help make your sentences longer and less choppy.

Short Sentences with Simple Predicates	Longer, Smoother Sentence with Compound Predicate
Bat opens her eyes. Bat twitches her ears.	Bat opens her eyes and twitches her ears.
My father saw a bat. My father took a picture of it.	My father saw a bat and took a picture of it.

Combine each pair of sentences. Use a compound predicate in each new sentence. Write the new sentence on the line.

1. I like to read about bats. I like to write stories about them.

____

2. The bat flew by the streetlight. The bat soared toward the pond.

____

3. My brother drew a picture of a bat. My brother gave it to me.

____

4. I found a book about bats in the library. I brought it home.

____

Name ______________________________ Date ____________

What Do Illustrators Do?
Phonics: Three-Letter Clusters (*scr, spr, str, thr*)

Write Words with Three-Letter Clusters

Read each question and choose an answer from the box. Write the word.

screwdriver	springtime	strongest
throne	scrubbing	unscramble
sprinkler	thrilling	streetlight

1. What do you call the person who can lift the heaviest load? ____________________
2. What lights the neighborhood on nights when there is no moon in the sky? ____________________
3. How would it feel to have an audience stand and applaud for you? ____________________
4. When do most trees grow new leaves? ____________________
5. What helps grass grow when there is no rain? ____________________
6. What is kept in a toolbox and can help put things together? ____________________
7. What is the best way to get dirty hands clean? ____________________
8. What is a queen's chair called? ____________________
9. How can you make a word from a set of mixed-up letters? ____________________

Name ______________________ Date ____________

Present and Past Tense

Many verbs in the **present tense** have an *-s* ending with a singular subject. Many verbs in the present tense do not have an *-s* ending with a plural subject. Most verbs in the **past tense** have an *-ed* ending.

An artist paints paintings.	present
Artists paint paintings.	present
An artist painted paintings yesterday.	past

Thinking Question
In what tense does the action of the verb occur, and what ending does the verb have?

Write *present* if the underlined verb shows the present tense. Write *past* if the underlined verb shows the past tense.

1. Our class gathers pages for a book. ____________
2. We combined them into a small book. ____________
3. We fold some pages in two. ____________
4. Other students traced lines for borders. ____________
5. Carmen cuts the rough edges. ____________
6. Walt and John iron the pages flat. ____________
7. Some older kids poked holes in the page.

   ____
8. One group ties string through the holes. ____________
9. The string pulled the pages together. ____________
10. In the last step, we cover it with thick paper.

    ____

Name ____________________ Date __________

Present, Past, and Future Tense

Many verbs in the **present tense** with singular subjects use an *-s* ending. Verbs in the present tense with plural subjects do not use an ending.

Many verbs in the **past tense** use an *-ed* ending.

Verbs in the **future tense** use the helping verb *will*.

The artist paints a curving line.	present
The artists paint a curving line.	present
The artist painted a curving line.	past
The artist will paint a curving line.	future

Thinking Question
In what tense does the action of the verb occur, and what ending does the verb have?

Write *present* if the underlined verb shows present tense. Write *past* if the underlined verb shows past tense. Write *future* if the underlined verb shows future tense.

1. My friends and I walked to the library. __________
2. We will search for interesting picture books. __________
3. Lora flips through many books. __________
4. Kitty stacked the books that we liked. __________
5. Roberto and Vera look for the best ones. __________
6. Quentin will place a marker at the colorful ones.

   ____
7. Tory loves art with bright colors. __________
8. Walt prefers art drawn with colored pencils. __________

Name ______________________ Date ____________

Spelling Word Sort

Write each Basic Word in the box where it belongs.

scr	*spr*

str	*thr*

Challenge: Add the Challenge Words to your Word Sort.

Spelling Words

Basic

1. three
2. scrap
3. street
4. spring
5. thrill
6. scream
7. strange
8. throw
9. string
10. scrape
11. spray
12. threw
13. strong
14. scratch

Review

think
they

Challenge

straight
scramble

Name ______________________ Date ____________

Focus Trait: Organization

Topic Sentence

Good writers of opinion paragraphs include a topic sentence that states an opinion. The topic sentence is followed by interesting details and reasons for the opinion. This makes an opinion stronger and more convincing. Compare the following sentences.

Weak Topic Sentence: Illustrators work on drawings.
Strong Topic Sentence: Illustrators often do very interesting work.

Read each paragraph. Revise the topic sentence in each paragraph to state an opinion.

1. Have you thought about composting leaves in the fall? That means you put the leaves in a pile instead of in the trash. The leaves eventually break down and can be added to gardening beds.

   ____

   ____

2. Many people exercise. Exercise helps people maintain a healthy weight. It also gives people more energy throughout the day.

   ____

   ____

Name ____________________ Date __________

Cumulative Review

Write words from the box to complete each paragraph.

threw	scratched	strong
screen	through	described
stretched	screamed	strange

Ray couldn't find the key to his house. He ________ (1) his head and tried to remember where he had seen it last. He went to the school office and ________ (2) his lost key chain. The clerk looked ________ (3) the Lost and Found box and found the key chain. Ray was grateful that someone had turned in his key!

***

Emily shivered as she looked out the window into the dark, foggy night. Suddenly she heard a ________ (4) noise coming from the back yard! She tiptoed to the back of the house and pushed open the ________ (5) door. She heard someone pound on the house and say, "Boo!" Emily ________ (6). Then her brother stepped into the light and they both laughed.

***

There was once a troll so mean and so tough that no one in the village was ________ (7) enough to fight him. The villagers ________ (8) out a huge net on the ground and hid next to their houses. When the troll came to town and stepped onto the net, the people wrapped him up, carried him out of town, and ________ (9) him into a big mud puddle. The troll never came back!

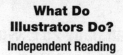

What Do Illustrators Do?

A Comic Book Guide to Illustrated Books

Now that you know what illustrators do, you can write about it in your own comic. Use examples from the text to help explain how an illustrated book is made.

Create a comic using the cat and the dog that watched as the illustrations were created.

Draw and write what illustrators do. Use details from page 246 for Step 1 and page 247 for Step 2.

Step 1

Step 2

What Do Illustrators Do?
Independent Reading

Name ______________________ Date ________

Read page 251. What do illustrators do to help them draw faces? Use what you learned to have the dog tell the cat two details from page 251 about drawing faces.

How Illustrators Draw Faces

Read page 258. In this comic, draw the cat talking about what she learned from the cover of *Jacqueline & the Magic Bean*. What does this cover tell you about the story?

Jacqueline & the Magic Bean

Name ________________________ Date ____________

Present, Past, and Future Tense

Write *present* if the underlined verb shows present tense. Write *past* if the underlined verb shows past tense.

1. Bill, the artist, selects a wall for art. ____________

2. He looked everywhere for a good wall. ____________

3. Some kids live near this wall. ____________

4. The owner allowed us to paint it. ____________

5. Bill climbs on a tall ladder. ____________

Write *present* if the underlined verb shows present tense. Write *past* if the underlined verb shows past tense. Write *future* if the underlined verb shows future tense.

6. The artist will measure the wall first. ____________

7. The colors drip down the wall. ____________

8. Someone else painted this wall long ago. ____________

9. When it is done, people will enjoy the wall. ____________

10. The new art stretches high into the sky. ____________

Name ______________________ Date ____________

Three-Letter Clusters

Write the Basic Word that is an antonym of the underlined word in each sentence.

1. Why did you choose such a <u>common</u> costume?
2. My uncle helped me learn how to <u>catch</u> a ball.
3. The <u>fall</u> is my favorite time of year.
4. Please <u>spread</u> the mud from your boots before coming in.
5. The surprise party was a big <u>bore</u> for me!
6. Are you <u>weak</u> enough to lift this heavy box?
7. Don't <u>whisper</u> in the library.
8. Everyone <u>caught</u> confetti to celebrate the new year.

1. ____________ 5. ____________

2. ____________ 6. ____________

3. ____________ 7. ____________

4. ____________ 8. ____________

Challenge: Write a word that means the opposite of each Challenge Word.

9. ____________________

10. ____________________

Use one of the Challenge Words and its antonym in a sentence.

11. ____________________

Spelling Words

Basic

1. three
2. scrap
3. street
4. spring
5. thrill
6. scream
7. strange
8. throw
9. string
10. scrape
11. spray
12. threw
13. strong
14. scratch

Review

think
they

Challenge

straight
scramble

Name ______________________ Date ____________

What Do Illustrators Do?
Vocabulary Strategies:
Synonyms

Synonyms

sketch	large	see	enormous
view	show	illustrate	exhibit
polite	pleasant		

Read each word below. Write the two synonyms from above that have almost the same meaning as the word.

1. display

____

2. huge

____

3. nice

____

4. observe

____

5. draw

____

Choose one set of synonyms. Write a sentence or two for each word to show the difference in the shades of meaning.

6. ____

____

____

____

____

Name ______________________ Date ____________

Kinds of Sentences

- There are four kinds of sentences.

The art is wonderful.	**Declarative** (statement)
Who made that piece?	**Interrogative** (question)
Pick up the mess you made.	**Imperative** (command)
What a bold color she used!	**Exclamatory** (exclamation)

Write *statement* if the sentence tells something. Write *question* if the sentence asks something.

1. We walked outside to paint. ______________

2. Who is going to come with us? ______________

3. Why are we going outside? ______________

Write *command* if the sentence tells someone to do something. Write *exclamation* if the sentence shows strong feeling.

4. Painting outside is fun! ______________

5. Do not spill paint out here. ______________

6. Create a painting with bold colors. ______________

Name ______________________________ Date ____________

What Do Illustrators Do?
Spelling:
Three-Letter Clusters

Proofreading for Spelling

Find the misspelled words and circle them.

War of the Giants

In the sterange world of the future, giant animals roam the earth. But what happens when the beasts come together in the last city on Earth? See these thee monsters clash in the biggest battle of all time!

Birdzilla This giant bird has claws srong enough to skratch through solid rock. It is headed steraight for the city!

The Ape King When angry, this towering ape can lift a car off the steet and thow it into the air. People skream and run. But can they get away?

The Night Croc This huge crocodile waits at the edge of town. When you least expect it, he will sping out of the dark and attack. This movie is filled with thills and surprises.

Don't Miss It!

Write the misspelled words correctly on the lines below.

1. ______________ 6. ______________
2. ______________ 7. ______________
3. ______________ 8. ______________
4. ______________ 9. ______________
5. ______________ 10. ______________

Spelling Words

Basic

1. three
2. scrap
3. street
4. spring
5. thrill
6. scream
7. strange
8. throw
9. string
10. scrape
11. spray
12. threw
13. strong
14. scratch

Review

think
they

Challenge

straight
scramble

Name ______________________ Date ____________

Connect to Writing

If all of the action in a paragraph happens during the same time, keep the verbs in the same tense.

Incorrect Paragraph

Next year, I will take an art class. Other students and I paint pictures of one another. We will study drawing and painting.

Correct Paragraph

Next year, I will take an art class. Other students and I will paint pictures of one another. We will study drawing and painting.

Read this paragraph. Change each underlined verb to make it match the tense of the other verbs. Write the new sentences on the lines below.

Maybe twenty years from now, cars will be very different than they are now. Drivers <u>enter</u> an address into a computer. The car will go to that place and the driver will be able to read or take a nap! Cars <u>serve</u> drinks and snacks. Cars <u>slow down</u> automatically when there is a stop sign ahead. All cars <u>run</u> on energy from the sun. Cars of the future <u>have</u> exciting features!

1. ______________________________

2. ______________________________

3. ______________________________

4. ______________________________

5. ______________________________

Name ______________________ Date __________

Write Words with Silent Letters *kn*, *wr*

Read each line of the poem. Choose the missing word from the box. Write the word.

wring	wrists	knight
wrapped	knot	wrong
kneel	wrinkles	knee

Handy Things to Remember

To keep a gift a secret, keep it ______(1)______ and out of sight.

To fight a pesky dragon, call a strong and fearless ______(2)______!

If one string isn't long enough, get two and make a ______(3)______.

To get the answers right, not ______(4)______, remember what you're taught.

To make a wet sponge dry, you need to ______(5)______ it out.

Hold it tightly with both hands and twist your ______(6)______ about.

Wear ______(7)______ pads when you're skating to keep from getting hurt.

To look your best, make sure there are no ______(8)______ in your shirt.

If you ______(9)______ in an anthill, stand up as quickly as you can.

If you forget these handy tips, just read them all again!

Name ______________________ Date ____________

Commas in a Series of Nouns

A series is a list of three or more words used in a sentence. Use **commas** to separate three or more nouns included in a series. Commas tell readers when to pause.

Juan grew beans, corn, and tomatoes.

Thinking Question
Are there three or more words listed together in the sentence?

Write each sentence correctly. Add commas where they are needed.

1. Jamal Tina and Ed want to write their own folktales.

   ____

2. Their class is having a contest for plays poems and folktales.

   ____

3. The friends read stories on Monday Tuesday and Wednesday.

   ____

4. Jamal read folktales about crows fish and cats.

   ____

5. Tina likes the folktales of England Spain and Mexico.

   ____

6. Folktales can take place in deserts jungles and cities.

   ____

Name _______________________ Date ___________

Commas in a Series of Verbs

A **series** is a list of three or more words used in a sentence. Use commas to separate three or more verbs included in a series. Commas tell readers when to pause.

Juan planted, watered, and harvested vegetables.

Thinking Question
Are there three or more words listed in the sentence?

Write each sentence correctly. Add commas where they are needed. If no commas are needed, write *No Commas* on the line.

1. I plan write and correct my folktale.

   ____

2. The animals in my story walk talk and snore.

   ____

3. My friends listened laughed and clapped as I read my story.

   ____

4. A snake trapped and tried to eat a frog in Ron's folktale.

   ____

5. The frog danced jumped and ran away from the snake.

   ____

Name ______________________ Date __________

Spelling Word Sort

Write each Basic Word in the web where it belongs.

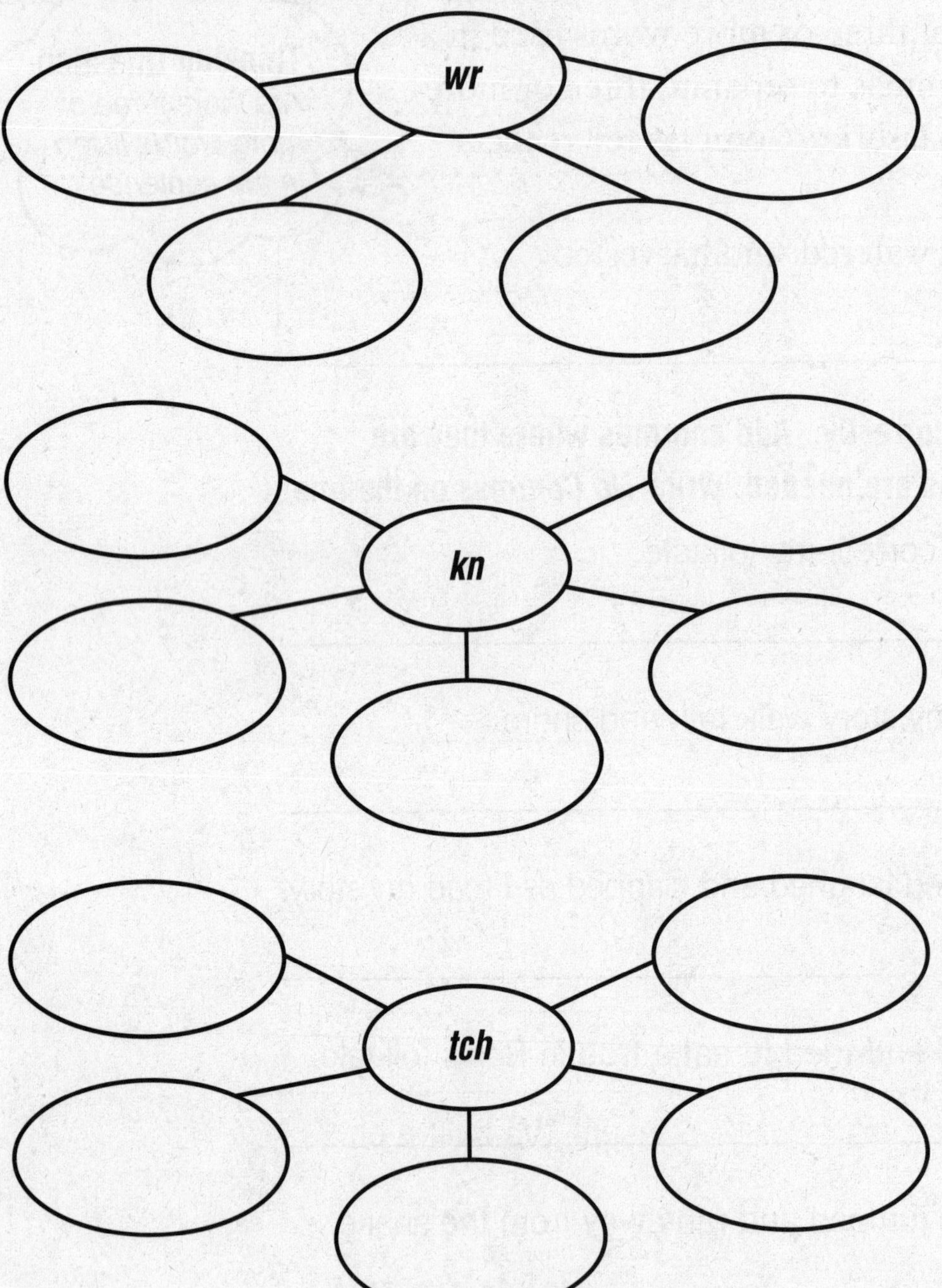

Spelling Words

Basic

1. itch
2. wreck
3. knee
4. patch
5. wrap
6. knot
7. watch
8. knife
9. stretch
10. write
11. knew
12. knock
13. match
14. wrong

Review

know
catch

Challenge

wrinkle
knuckle

Challenge: Add the Challenge Words to your Word Sort. Write each one near the correct group, and draw a line to connect it to the web.

Name ______________________ Date __________

Focus Trait: Word Choice

Using Linking Words

Linking words and phrases can connect supporting reasons to opinions in a paragraph. This makes the author's ideas easier to understand.

Linking Words	
because therefore	since for example

Rewrite each passage so a linking word or phrase connects the reason to the opinion.

1. The male peacock is the most beautiful bird. It has shimmering purple and green feathers.

2. Our zoo has animals from many places. It has rare orangutans, pandas, and polar bears.

3. The garden in our back yard is unusual. We built it on a hill.

4. Our pumpkin was the best in the fair. It won first place.

Name _______________________ Date ____________

Cumulative Review

Write words from the box to complete the lines of the play.

know	wrong	wrote
threw	knees	through
knickknacks	wrap	knocked

Granny and the Rascal

Granny Gopher: Who ______________ over my beautiful vase?

Rascal Raccoon: Why are you so upset about a silly old vase? You have plenty of other ______________ sitting around.

Granny Gopher: That vase was special. Great-Granny Gopher gave it to me. Now, is there something you'd like to confess?

Rascal Raccoon: I ______________ that you think I broke that vase, but I never went near it.

Granny Gopher: That's what you said after you ______________ a baseball ______________ my window.

Rascal Raccoon: You were ______________ about that, too.

Granny Gopher: There were witnesses to that crime. Skunk and Rabbit ______________ me a note saying they *saw* you break the window.

Rascal Raccoon: You can't trust what those tattle-tales say!

Granny Gopher: You can at least clean up this broken glass. It's hard for me to get down on my sore old ______________ to do a job like this.

Rascal Raccoon: Uh, sure, Granny Gopher. I have to ______________ a present for Rabbit's birthday party right now. But I'll stop by and help you later. *I promise!*

Name ______________________________ Date ______

The Harvest Birds

A Radio Interview

The harvest birds have come in for a special radio interview. They saw everything that happened to Juan Zanate, and they are ready to tell his story. Use details from the text to answer the interviewer's questions.

Read pages 285–292.

Interviewer: Juan Zanate was looking for land for a long time. Finally, Grandpa Chon agreed to give him some. You were there and saw what happened next. Please explain what happened.

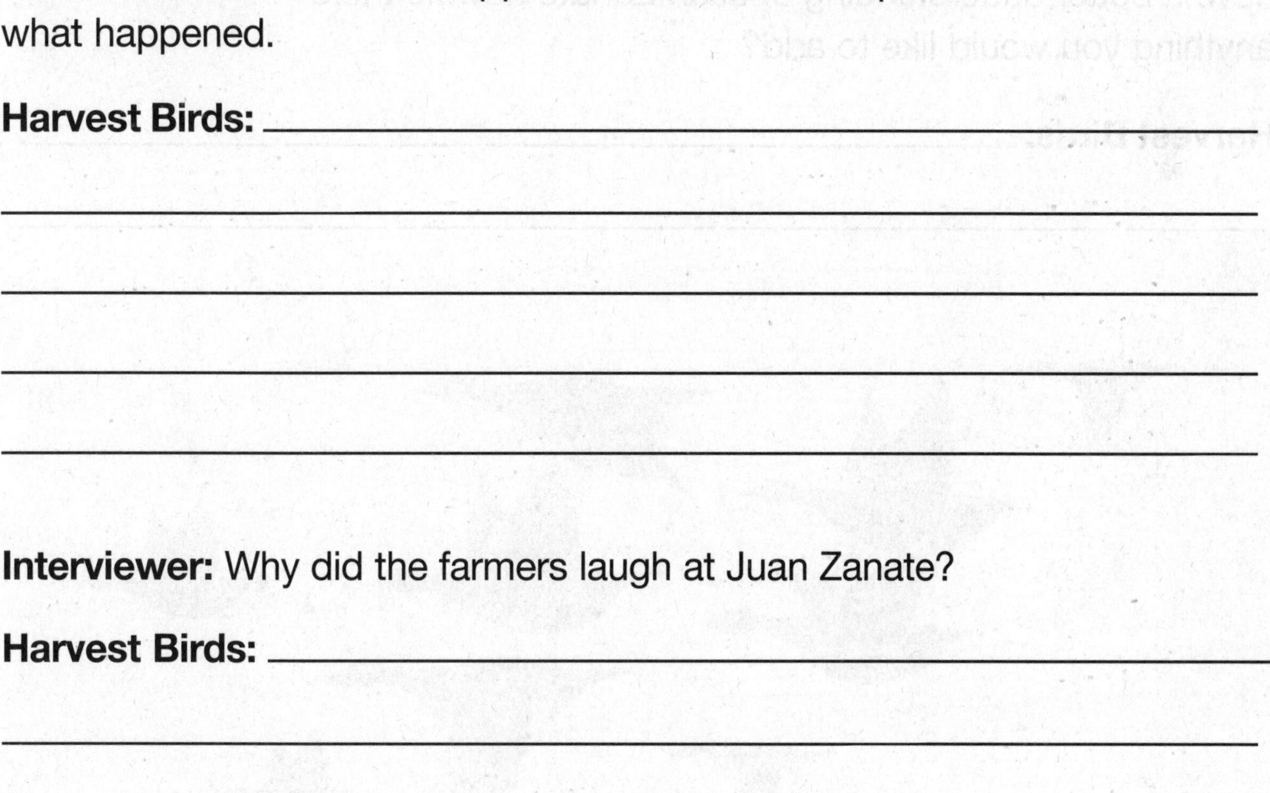

Harvest Birds: ______________________________

____

____

____

____

Interviewer: Why did the farmers laugh at Juan Zanate?

Harvest Birds: ______________________________

____

____

____

Name ______________________________ Date ________

Read pages 293–297.

Interviewer: Juan had a great harvest at the end of the summer. How did people react to this?

Harvest Birds: ____

____

Interviewer: Now just between us, what is your secret?

Harvest Birds: ____

____

Interviewer: Well, thank you, harvest birds! I think we have a better understanding of Juan Zanate now. Is there anything you would like to add?

Harvest Birds: ____

____

Name ______________________ Date __________

Commas in Addresses

- Use a comma to separate each part of an address.

  Susan Henley, 29 Wylie Lane, Ocoee, Florida

Write each address correctly. Add commas where they are needed.

1. Tammy Ruiz 14 Silver Brook Road Dallas Texas

   ____

2. Wayne Thomas 1170 South Pleasant Street Belding Michigan

   ____

3. The package is going to Dave Layler 73 Bent Road Remsen New York.

   ____

4. My friend lives at 87 Moore Avenue Glendale California.

   ____

5. We are moving to 60 Myrtle Street Addis Louisiana.

   ____

6. The letter is from Lucy Rawly 170 Adobe Way Albuquerque New Mexico.

   ____

Name ______________________ Date ____________

Unexpected Consonant Spellings

Write the Basic Word that best completes each sentence.

1. Your elbow and your ______________ are both body parts that can bend.
2. A pair of scissors and a ______________ are both tools for cutting.
3. To share a story, you can tell it to someone or ______________ it down.
4. Two things that can have a flame are a candle and a ______________.
5. To tell the time, you can look at a clock or check your ______________.
6. To let someone know you're at the door, ring the bell or ______________.
7. You can tie a bow or just tie a ______________.
8. A rubber band and bubble gum are both things that can ______________.

Challenge: Name something that is similar to a knuckle. Then write to tell how the two things are alike.

9. ______________

10. ____

____

Spelling Words

Basic

1. itch
2. wreck
3. knee
4. patch
5. wrap
6. knot
7. watch
8. knife
9. stretch
10. write
11. knew
12. knock
13. match
14. wrong

Review

know
catch

Challenge

wrinkle
knuckle

Name ______________________ Date ____________

Context Clues

Read each sentence. Use context clues to figure out the meaning of the underlined word. Use a dictionary to check that your meanings are correct.

1. Did you note our meeting on your calendar?

   ____

2. We needed another yard of yarn to finish the sewing project.

   ____

3. I didn't win, but I didn't feel bitter about it.

   ____

4. She always hangs up her coat, so it was odd that she misplaced it.

   ____

5. The shallow bowl only held a little bit of water.

   ____

6. Tina was mortified when she fell in front of the school.

   ____

Name ______________________ Date ____________

Sentence Fragments

- A **sentence** is a group of words that tells a complete thought. It tells who or what, and it tells an action or state of being.

  A man planted seeds in his garden.

Write the group of words that will complete each sentence.

1. A bird ______________________.

   lives in the tree   **on the fence**

2. Rabbits ______________________.

   soft and cute   **like to eat garden vegetables**

3. ______________________ are vegetable eaters.

   Rabbits   **Usually**

4. ______________________ ate the whole garden of flowers.

   Broke through a fence   **A herd of goats**

For each item, combine the two fragments to write a complete sentence.

5. A bird is. a clever but shy animal.

   ____

6. A garden needs. a fence that can keep animals out.

   ____

Name ______________________ Date __________

Proofreading for Spelling

The Harvest Birds
Spelling:
Unexpected Consonant Spellings

Find the misspelled words and circle them.

Lost Hiker Rescued on Big Pine Trail

Thanks to her own quick thinking, 10-year-old Rosa Gomez was rescued along Big Pine Trail on Saturday. The girl had stopped to wach a group of deer and lost her hiking group. She tried to catch up but took the rong trail. Rosa new she was lost and wanted to leave clues to help someone find her. She decided to rite her name in the dirt with a stick each time she took a turn. The girl had to stop after she fell on a rocky area. Her nuckles were scraped and her nee was badly cut. To stop the bleeding, Rosa used her pocket nife to cut a strip from her sweatshirt. She used the cloth to rap the injury and tie a not just as she had learned to do in first-aid training. The minutes began to strech into hours, but Rosa stayed calm. Rescuers found her just before dark.

Spelling Words

1. itch
2. wreck
3. knee
4. patch
5. wrap
6. knot
7. watch
8. knife
9. stretch
10. write
11. knew
12. knock
13. match
14. wrong

Review

know
catch

Challenge

wrinkle
knuckle

Write the misspelled words correctly on the lines below.

1. ______________ 6. ______________

2. ______________ 7. ______________

3. ______________ 8. ______________

4. ______________ 9. ______________

5. ______________ 10. ______________

Name ______________________ Date __________

Connect to Writing

You can combine short, choppy sentences to make your writing smoother. You can combine sentences by **joining single words in a series.** You use commas to separate the nouns or verbs in a series. Remember to add *and* after the last comma.

Short, Choppy Sentences	Longer, Smoother Sentence
Carla watched crows. Carla watched gulls. Carla watched pigeons.	Carla watched crows, gulls, and pigeons.

Combine three short, choppy sentences by joining nouns or verbs in a series. Write the new sentence on the line.

1.

The crows in the story walked.	The crows in the story laughed.	The crows in the story talked.

____

2.

Carla told Ramon about the crows.	Carla told Ed about the crows.	Carla told Lisa about the crows.

____

3.

The crows perched on branches.	The crows perched on wires.	The crows perched on rooftops.

____

4.

Ramon played with the birds.	Ramon laughed with the birds.	Ramon sang with the birds.

____

Name ______________________ Date ____________

Kamishibai Man
Phonics: Vowel Diphthongs *ow* and *ou*

Words with Diphthongs *ow* and *ou*

Read each sentence. Choose the missing word from the box. Write the word.

crowded	rowdy	outdoors
found	showers	sunflower
howling	doghouse	shouted

1. As soon as the rain stopped, the children hurried ______________ to play.
2. When a wolf is ______________, you can hear it from far away.
3. Our poodle Fifi sleeps in her ______________, where it is warm and dry.
4. When the birthday girl came in, everyone jumped up and ______________, "Surprise!"
5. Will it be sunny today, or will we have ______________?
6. The ______________ seeds that we planted grew into tall plants with bright yellow blooms.
7. Carl still hasn't ______________ the jacket that he lost last month.
8. The bus was so ______________ that a lot of riders had to stand up.
9. If the children get too ______________, they might wake the baby.

Name ______________________ Date ____________

Kamishibai Man
Grammar: Abstract Nouns

Abstract Nouns

- A **noun** can name a person, place, or thing. This kind of noun is a **concrete noun**.
- A noun can also name an idea, a feeling, or a quality. This is called an **abstract noun**. You cannot see, hear, taste, smell, or touch an abstract noun.

  He listened in the hope of hearing a new story.

  It was just luck that he arrived in time.

Thinking Questions
Does the noun name an idea, a feeling, or a quality?

A noun in each sentence is underlined. Write *abstract* if the noun names an idea, a feeling, or a quality. Write *concrete* if it is a noun you can see, hear, taste, smell, or touch.

1. The younger men enjoyed the older man's friendship.

   ____

2. The old man found strength in being among friends.

   ____

3. The friends took delight in listening to the old man's stories. ______________

4. One story was about a silly king. ______________

5. The crowd's laughter pleased the old man. ______________

6. It gave him energy to tell another story.

   ____

Name ______________________ Date ____________

Abstract Nouns

A noun that names an idea, a feeling, or a quality is an **abstract noun**. You cannot see, hear, taste, smell, or touch an abstract noun.

The couple did not have much wealth.

Their joy was obvious for everyone to see.

Thinking Question
Does the noun name an idea, a feeling, or a quality?

The word in parentheses tells whether the abstract noun in the sentence names an idea, a feeling, or a quality. Write the noun.

1. He took delight in keeping the audience in suspense.

   (feeling) ______________

2. He told the story with complete honesty.

   (quality) ______________

Write a sentence for each abstract noun.

3. beauty

   ____

   ____

4. childhood

   ____

   ____

Name ______________________ Date __________

The Kamishibai Man
Spelling:
Vowel Sound in *town*

Spelling Word Sort

Write each Basic Word in the correct list.

mouth	down

Challenge: Add the Challenge Words to your Word Sort.

Spelling Words

Basic

1. clown
2. round
3. bow
4. cloud
5. power
6. crown
7. thousand
8. crowd
9. sound
10. count
11. powder
12. blouse
13. frown
14. pound

Review

house
found

Challenge

mountain
coward

Name ______________________ Date ____________

Kamishibai Man
Writing:
Opinion Writing

Focus Trait: Organization
Opinion Statement

When a question asks for your opinion, begin your answer by stating your opinion clearly. Use words from the question in your opinion statement.

EXAMPLE:
Question: In *Kamishibai Man,* why do you think the old man and his wife call each other "Grandma" and "Grandpa" although they have no children of their own?
Strong Opening: I think the old man and his wife call each other "Grandma" and "Grandpa" because they wish they had children and grandchildren.

Read each question about *Kamishibai Man.* Write a strong opening sentence that clearly states your opinion. Use words from the question in your statement.

1. **Question:** Why do you think the children were always happy to see the kamishibai man?

   Opinion Statement:

2. **Question:** How do you think the kamishibai man felt when he returned to the city?

   Opinion Statement:

3. **Question:** Why do you think the little boy ran away from the kamishibai man?

   Opinion Statement:

Name ______________________ Date ____________

Cumulative Review

Write a word from the box to complete each rhyme.

clown	cow	kneel	pout	wreck
count	crown	knight	powder	write

1. You're going to have to ______________ to change that wheel.

2. A princess wears a gown with her ______________.

3. Please add some chili ______________ to the chowder.

4. Why would you paint a frown on a ______________?

5. You won't see that ______________ lose a fight.

6. When you're dressed as a scout, do not ______________.

7. The lady hurt her neck in the ______________.

8. Be careful with that plow around the ______________.

9. You should get this amount when you ______________.

10. Before you start to ______________, turn on a light.

Name ______________________ Date ________

Kamishibai Man

A New Point of View: The Boy Who Didn't Like Candy

When I was a boy, I listened to the stories of the kamishibai man every day. Help me tell his story with details from the text and illustrations.

Read pages 324–326. Why was the old man surprised?

____

____

____

____

Read pages 328–330. Why was the old man happy?

____

____

____

Name ______________________ Date ______

Read page 332. Why did I run away from the kamishibai man when I was a little boy?

____

____

____

Read page 333–334. How did television change things?

____

____

____

Read page 338. What happened when the large crowd gathered?

____

____

____

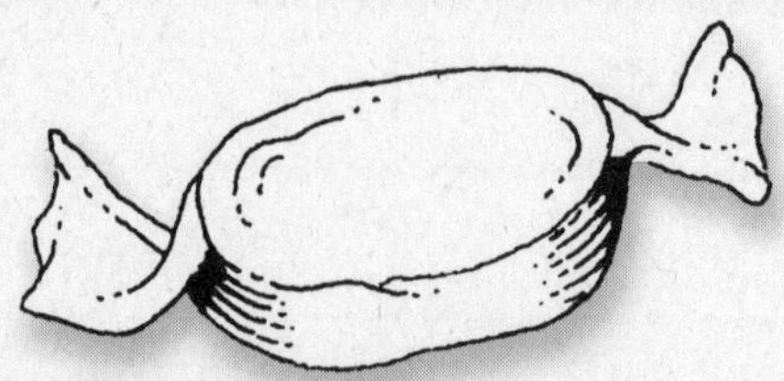

Name ____________________ Date ____________

Abstract Nouns

- The subject of a sentence is a noun. It can be concrete or abstract.
- A noun that names an idea, a feeling, or a quality is an **abstract noun**.

In the story, the girls formed a friendship.

Two nouns in each sentence are underlined. Circle the subject of the sentence. Write the abstract noun.

1. The story begins with memories of a missing locket.

____

2. A letter had information about the locket.

____

3. The girls had confidence in themselves.

____

4. After several hours, Annette had success and found the locket. ____________________

Choose two abstract nouns from above and write a sentence with them.

5. ____

____

Name ______________________ Date ____________

Vowel Sound in *town*

Write the Basic Word that best replaces the underlined word or words in each sentence.

1. The man wears a ring of gold and jewels on his head to show he is king.
2. The actress waved to the large group of people as she walked by.
3. The angry bees made a loud buzzing noise.
4. Her brother's teasing made Marta put an unhappy look on her face.
5. Let's say the numbers in order as Justin jumps the rope.
6. A performer in a silly costume gave out balloons to all the children.
7. That gray puffy shape in the sky looks like it might bring rain.
8. For my birthday, I had a circle-shaped cake decorated to look like a soccer ball.

1. ______________
2. ______________
3. ______________
4. ______________
5. ______________
6. ______________
7. ______________
8. ______________

Spelling Words

Basic

1. clown
2. round
3. bow
4. cloud
5. power
6. crown
7. thousand
8. crowd
9. sound
10. count
11. powder
12. blouse
13. frown
14. pound

Review

house
found

Challenge

mountain
coward

Challenge: On another sheet of paper, write a one-paragraph story using both Challenge Words and one or more Basic Words.

Name ______________________ Date ____________

Dictionary/Glossary

Read each word. Find each word in a print or digital dictionary. Complete the chart.

Word	Part(s) of Speech	Word with Endings
1. jewel		
2. rickety		
3. blast		
4. sharp		
5. blur		

Now write one sentence of your own that could be an example sentence for one meaning of each word.

1. ______________________________

2. ______________________________

3. ______________________________

4. ______________________________

5. ______________________________

Name ______________________ Date ____________

Writing Titles and Addresses

Kamishibai Man
Grammar:
Spiral Review

- Begin the first, last, and each important word in a book or story title with a capital letter. Example: Reptiles on the Road
- Capitalize a person's title when it is in front of his or her name. Example: Detective Ruiz
- Use a comma to separate each part of an address. Example: Ken Lopez, 530 Sandy Lane, Hialeah, Florida

Capitalize each title correctly.

1. I checked out swimming with the dolphins from the library.

    ____

2. He listened to coach Taylor speak.

    ____

3. Her story is called "never listen to a gerbil."

    ____

4. The book a great leader is about president Washington.

    ____

Write each address correctly. Add commas where they are needed.

5. Sam Johnson 22 Meadowlark Avenue Houston Texas

    ____

6. She moved to 749 South Lake Road Spokane Washington.

    ____

Name ______________________ Date ____________

Kamishibai Man
Spelling:
Vowel Sound in *town*

Proofreading for Spelling

Find the misspelled words and circle them.

Dear Uncle Tony,

Thanks for the circus tickets that you sent. I can always cownt on you to make my birthday a lot of fun! I really enjoyed the elephant act. The biggest one must have weighed a thausand pownds.

The acrobat show was great, too. No one made a sownd while one acrobat carried his partner over the tightrope. When they came down, they leaped through a rownd hoop that was on fire. The crawd went crazy! Then, a cloun pretended he was going to do the same thing, but he was too scared. His buddies laughed at him as if he was a big couward. Finally, he jumped through the hoop and his pants caught fire. When he took his bouw, he saw the clowd of smoke behind him. It was really funny.

I hope that next time you come to town, we can all go to the circus together!

Love,
Gina

Spelling Words

Basic

1. clown
2. round
3. bow
4. cloud
5. power
6. crown
7. thousand
8. crowd
9. sound
10. count
11. powder
12. blouse
13. frown
14. pound

Review

house
found

Challenge

mountain
coward

Write the misspelled words correctly on the lines below.

1. ______________ 6. ______________
2. ______________ 7. ______________
3. ______________ 8. ______________
4. ______________ 9. ______________
5. ______________ 10. ______________

Name ______________________ Date ____________

Connect to Writing

Exact nouns are used to make your writing clearer and more interesting.

Noun	Exact Noun
The story filled Linda with happiness.	The story filled Linda with delight.
His actions showed his kindness.	His actions showed his compassion.

Replace each underlined noun in the sentences with a more exact noun. Use the nouns in the word box.

joy	doubt
panic	bravery

1. Jen felt uncertainty about telling her story to strangers.

   ____

2. Her fear grew as more people arrived. ________________
3. Seeing her best friend in the audience gave her courage.

   ____

4. In the story, the characters felt happiness about the coming circus. ________________

Name ______________________ Date __________

Write Words with *au*, *aw*, *al*, and *o*

Read each sentence and choose an answer from the box. Write the word. Then read the sentence aloud.

tablecloth	yawning	offered
sauce	faucet	bossy
false	awesome	mall

1. To save water, be sure to fix a leaky ______________ as soon as possible.
2. We went shopping at the ______________ and had lunch at the Food Court.
3. My ______________ cousin Cindy makes her brothers do everything her way.
4. Pete had homemade yogurt with raspberry ______________ on top.
5. On our test, we had to tell whether each statement was true or ______________.
6. The desert sunset was an ______________ sight!
7. Coach Simms ______________ to help me work on my pitch.
8. The gravy spilled and stained our best ______________.
9. Are the girls ______________ because they are tired or because they are bored?

Name ______________________ Date ____________

Subject Pronouns

A **pronoun** is a word that can take the place of one or more nouns in a sentence. The pronouns *I*, *you*, *he*, *she*, *it*, *we*, and *they* are **subject pronouns**. Pronouns can be singular or plural. A noun and the subject pronoun that replaces it must match each other in singular and plural forms.

The telegraph was important.	It was important.
Samuel Morse invented it.	He invented it.
Our class learned this.	We learned this.

Thinking Question
What pronoun can replace and match a noun or nouns in a sentence?

Write each sentence. Replace the underlined word or words with a subject pronoun.

1. Samuel Morse was born in Massachusetts.

____

2. Lucretia Walker became his wife.

____

3. The couple had two children.

____

4. Painting was another thing Morse did well.

____

5. The students and I enjoyed learning about him.

____

Name ______________________________ Date ______________

Object Pronouns

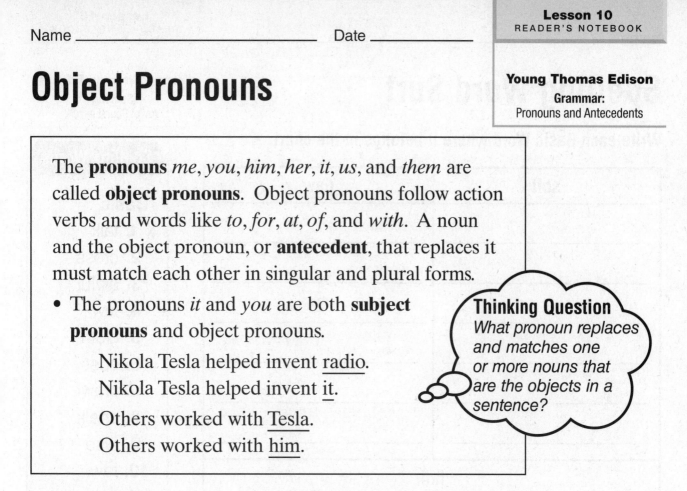

The **pronouns** *me*, *you*, *him*, *her*, *it*, *us*, and *them* are called **object pronouns**. Object pronouns follow action verbs and words like *to*, *for*, *at*, *of*, and *with*. A noun and the object pronoun, or **antecedent**, that replaces it must match each other in singular and plural forms.

- The pronouns *it* and *you* are both **subject pronouns** and object pronouns.

  Nikola Tesla helped invent radio.
  Nikola Tesla helped invent it.

  Others worked with Tesla.
  Others worked with him.

Thinking Question
What pronoun replaces and matches one or more nouns that are the objects in a sentence?

Write each sentence. Replace the underlined word or words with an object pronoun.

1. A man named Marconi worked on wireless communication.

   ____

2. He helped make radios popular.

   ____

3. Marconi married Beatrice O'Brien in 1905.

   ____

4. Other people said they had invented the system.

   ____

5. People are grateful to Marconi for what he did.

   ____

Name ______________________ Date ____________

Spelling Word Sort

Write each Basic Word where it belongs in the chart.

s**o**ft	p**aw**
________	________
________	________
________	________
________	________
________	________
________	________

f**a**ll
____
____
____
____
____
____

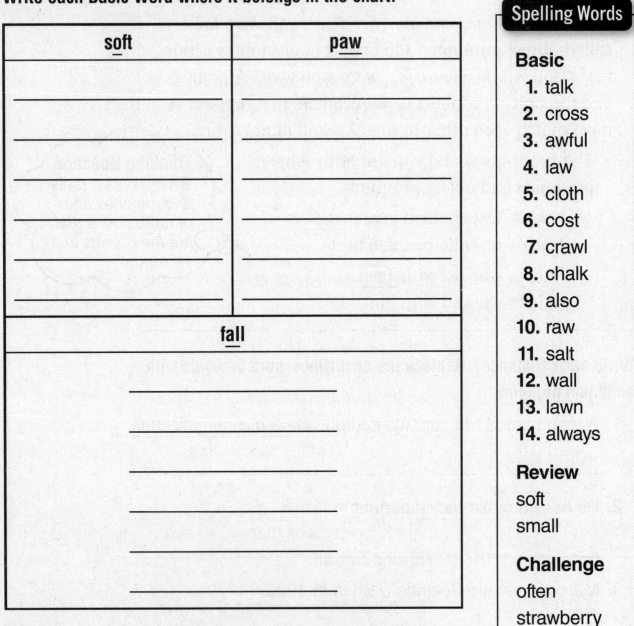

Challenge: Add the Challenge Words to your Word Sort.

Spelling Words

Basic

1. talk
2. cross
3. awful
4. law
5. cloth
6. cost
7. crawl
8. chalk
9. also
10. raw
11. salt
12. wall
13. lawn
14. always

Review

soft
small

Challenge

often
strawberry

Focus Trait: Sentence Fluency
Avoiding Redundancy

Good writers introduce a new idea in each sentence. This writer crossed out a sentence that repeats an idea and wrote a new idea.

Thomas Edison loved to read. He would spend the entire day at the library. He wanted to read every book in the library. He would start at the last book on the shelf and work back to the first. ~~Edison wanted to read all of the books there~~.

New idea: *He would dream about his next experiment as he read.*

Read each paragraph. Cross out the sentence that repeats an idea. Write a new idea.

1. Thomas Edison was a very creative child. He created a laboratory in the cellar of his home. He would mix chemicals there. He would do this in the cellar. He also asked questions so that he could learn about things.

   New Idea: ______________________________

2. Edison's mother was important in his life. She educated him at home. She taught him very well there. She also encouraged him to learn for himself.

   New Idea: ______________________________

3. Edison invented many helpful things. He invented the carbon transmitter, which made voices sound louder. He invented the light bulb. This invention helped people. He even invented the motion picture.

   New Idea: ______________________________

   ____

Name ______________________ Date ____________

Cumulative Review

Write words from the box to complete the sentences.

cause	walkie-talkies	squawked
officer	foggy	already
paws	fault	flossing

1. My friend and I used ________________ to communicate.

2. Brushing and ________________ keep teeth healthy.

3. The chicken ________________ loudly and flapped its wings.

4. The police ________________ directed traffic when the lights were not working.

5. Dr. Ross finally figured out the ________________ of the baby's fever.

6. When Tasha arrived, the game had ________________ started.

7. It was so ________________ that I could barely see my neighbor's house.

8. It was my ________________ that the library book got torn.

9. The kitten is all black except for its four white ________________.

Name ______________________ Date ________

Young Thomas Edison

A Tour of the Thomas Edison Museum

Welcome to the Thomas Edison Museum! I am a tour guide for the museum. Help me take our visitors on a tour. We will explore Thomas Edison's early life by looking at some objects.

Read page 362.

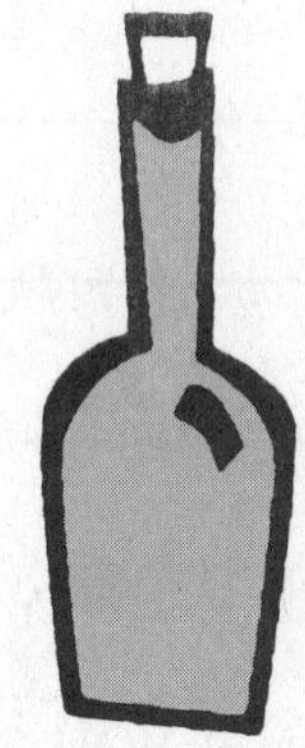

This is a bottle from Thomas Edison's childhood. Why is it here in the museum?

____

____

____

Read page 366.

Here you can see an old newspaper from when Thomas Edison was twelve years old. Why is it here in the museum?

____

____

____

Name ______________________ Date ________

Read page 372.

Here is a photograph of an old locomotive. Why is it in the Thomas Edison museum?

____

____

____

Read page 376.

Here is the last letter Thomas Edison received from his mother in 1869. Why is it here?

____

____

____

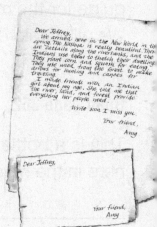

Read pages 379–381.

Now if you step into the final room of the museum, you will see all of Thomas Edison's famous inventions! Why was he known as "The Wizard"?

____

____

____

Thank you for taking a tour of the Thomas Edison Museum. It has been my pleasure to be your guide!

Name ______________________ Date ____________

Pronoun-Antecedent Agreement

- A pronoun can take the place of one or more nouns in a sentence.
- An **antecedent** is the noun or noun phrase to which a pronoun refers. An antecedent usually comes before the pronoun, but it may come after. Pronouns and antecedents must agree in number, person, and gender.

  Raul thought about his invention.

  Maggie thought about her invention.

  Raul and Maggie thought about their inventions.

Complete each sentence by writing the pronoun that agrees with the underlined antecedent. Remember to make sure the pronoun and antecedent match in number, person, and gender.

1. Kevin checked out an invention book because __________ had a lot of information.
2. I said, "Show __________ the book."
3. Maggie typed up the notes __________ wrote about the invention.
4. The students felt __________ had done a great job.
5. Ms. Jones said __________ was proud of the students' hard work.
6. After __________ was done, Raul went home.

Name ____________________ Date __________

Vowel Sound in *talk*

Read the titles and lists below. Write the Basic Word that belongs in each blank.

1. Things to Look for Before You ____________: cars, trucks, bicycles
2. Ways to Communicate: draw a picture, use sign language, ____________
3. Writing Tools: pencil, pen, ____________
4. Things That Are Against the ____________: littering, speeding, stealing
5. Spices and Seasonings: garlic, cinnamon, ____________
6. Things People Eat ____________: apples, lettuce, tomatoes
7. Parts of a Building: staircase, window, ____________
8. Things Made of ____________: shirt, scarf, sheet

Challenge: Write two lists similar to those above. Include a Challenge Word in each title or list.

Spelling Words

Basic

1. talk
2. cross
3. awful
4. law
5. cloth
6. cost
7. crawl
8. chalk
9. also
10. raw
11. salt
12. wall
13. lawn
14. always

Review

soft
small

Challenge

often
strawberry

Name ______________________ Date ____________

Shades of Meaning

For each set of related words, write them in order on the arrows to show the shades of meanings of the words. If necessary, look up unfamiliar words in a dictionary before completing the arrows.

1. believe, suspect, think

←——————————————————————→

2. happy, elated, content

←——————————————————————→

3. angry, upset, furious, annoyed

←——————————————————————→

4. scorching, hot, warm

←——————————————————————→

5. glance, look, glare, stare

←——————————————————————→

6. excited, exhilarated, enthusiastic

←——————————————————————→

Name _______________ Date _______________

Singular and Plural Nouns

- A noun that names only one person, place, or thing is a **singular noun**.
- A noun that names more than one person, place, or thing is a **plural noun**.
- Add *-s* to most singular nouns to form the plural.
- Add *-es* to form the plural of a singular noun that ends in *-s*, *-sh*, *-ch*, or *-x*.

  Students have invented things for many of their school classes.

Write singular or plural for each underlined noun.

1. An invention is like a lightbulb lighting up in your head.

   ____

2. Before, my thoughts were in the dark. _______________
3. I don't know how a new idea comes to me. _______________
4. I phoned two friends about my idea. _______________
5. I will give them two guesses about what it is.

   ____

Use proofreading marks to change the underlined nouns from singular nouns to plural nouns.

Thank you for the idea box that you sent. We should meet to talk about the invention we are thinking about. I shared your thought with my brother.

Name ________________________ Date ____________

Proofreading for Spelling

Young Thomas Edison
Spelling:
Vowel Sound in *talk*

Find the misspelled words and circle them.

This morning was auful. I wanted to sleep late, but my brother kept whining. He was crawss because Mom wouldn't let him go out and play unless I went with him. I olways have to babysit! All I wanted was a little sleep. Since when is that against the lauw? Anyway, I took Ben out to play. I stretched out on the laun to relax, but before long Ben just had to crol over and bug me. He doesn't tawk very well yet, but I know what "jump game" means. Ben auften watches me play hopscotch and thinks it looks funny. I got some chawk and drew a board on the sidewalk. Ben laughed when I hopped on the squares. Then he was bored again. He wanted to swing. He aulso wanted a drink of water. When Ben finally took his nap, I ran to Ana's house. I'm going to sleep over tonight. Maybe I'll get to sleep late at *her* house!

Spelling Words

Basic

1. talk
2. cross
3. awful
4. law
5. cloth
6. cost
7. crawl
8. chalk
9. also
10. raw
11. salt
12. wall
13. lawn
14. always

Review

soft
small

Challenge

often
strawberry

Write the misspelled words correctly on the lines below.

1. ____________ 6. ____________
2. ____________ 7. ____________
3. ____________ 8. ____________
4. ____________ 9. ____________
5. ____________ 10. ____________

Name ______________________ Date __________

Connect to Writing

Using a pronoun in place of a noun helps to avoid repeating words.

Repeated Nouns	Better Sentences
In 1806,Thomas Young thought of the phonograph. Later, Leon Scott improved the phonograph. Thomas Edison made the phonograph work.	In 1806,Thomas Young thought of the phonograph. Later, Leon Scott improved it. Thomas Edison made it work.

Rewrite each item. Use pronouns in place of repeated nouns.

1. The first phonograph did not play records. The first phonograph put sounds on a tin tube. Sounds entered the first phonograph through a bell.

____

____

2. Later, phonographs played records. These records were flat rings of wax. A needle cut sound into the records.

____

____

3. Bell and Tainter made their phonograph in 1886. Bell and Tainter called their phonograph a gramophone. The government gave its approval to Bell and Tainter.

____

____

____

Name ______________________ Date ________

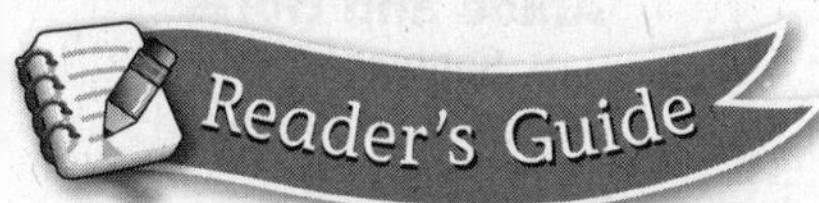

Amos and Boris

Postcard to Pearl

Help Amos send a postcard to his friend, Pearl, telling her about his travel plans. Use the text and illustrations to describe the most important details about Amos and his boat. Then, use this information to write the postcard.

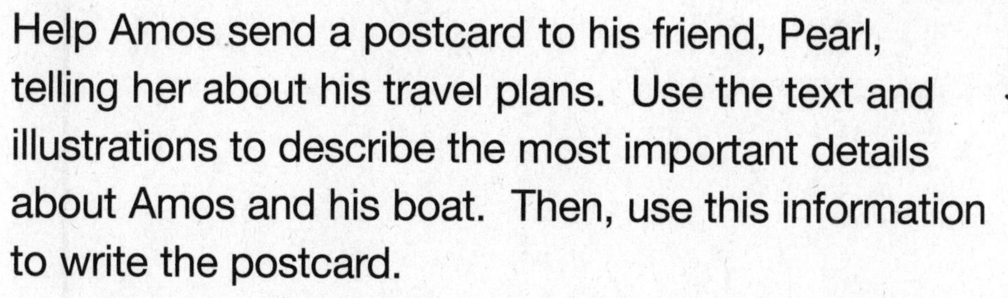

Read pages 3–5. Why did Amos love where he lived?

____

____

Why did Amos decide to build a boat?

____

____

What did Amos do when the boat was finished, before setting sail?

____

____

How do you think Amos felt before setting sail?

____

____

Name ______________________________ Date ______

Now, use your answers to write the postcard. On the front, draw a picture of Amos and his boat. On the back, write a note from Amos to Pearl. Describe his plans for the boat and where he wants to go.

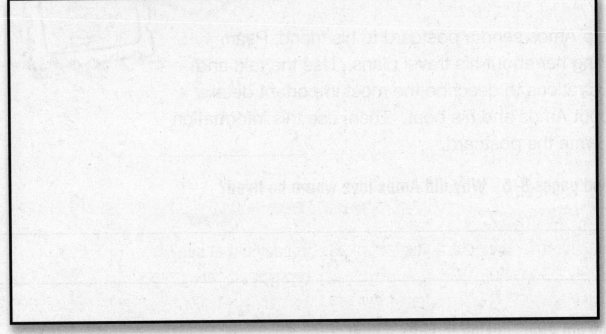

Front of Postcard

Dear Pearl,

____

____

____

____

____

____

____

Love, Amos

32¢

TO:

Pearl M. Friend

333 Cheddar Street

Cheesetown, USA

Back of Postcard

Name ______________________________ Date ________

From Amos's Journal

Amos kept a journal during his time on the boat. Use the text and illustrations to help fill out his journal entries.

Read page 6. What was the weather like when Amos started out? How did he feel at first?

September 6

____

____

Read page 7. How did Amos feel on his first day out at sea?

September 7

____

____

How did Amos feel after the first day?

September 8

____

____

Name ______________________ Date ________

Read page 9. What are some things Amos saw while lying on the deck of his boat?

September 9

____

____

How did Amos feel when he was lying on the deck of his boat?

Later that night …

____

____

What do you think Amos's last thoughts were before he unexpectedly fell into the sea? Write his final journal entry.

Even later that night …

____

____

Name ______________________ Date ______

Message in a Bottle

Imagine that Amos found his pen and paper with him in the water. Quickly, he wrote a message for help and put it in a bottle. First, use the text and illustrations to explain what happened. Then use that information to write Amos's message in a bottle.

Read page 9. How did Amos fall off his boat?

____

____

Read page 10. What did Amos do when he first fell off the boat?

____

____

Read page 11. What happened to Amos next?

____

____

What was Amos worried about?

____

____

Name ______________________ Date ______

Use your answers to write Amos's message in a bottle. Describe what happened to him and why he needs help.

Name ______________________ Date ______

Amos and Boris

Best Friend Award

After his adventures with Boris, Amos decided to give Boris a Best Friend Award.

Read page 12.
How did Amos feel before Boris found him?

____

____

Read pages 13–15.
How did Amos feel when he first met Boris?

____

____

Read pages 18–19.
What was it like for Amos traveling on Boris's back?

____

____

Read page 20.
How did Amos feel when it was time to say goodbye to Boris?

____

____

Name ______________________ Date ________

Design a Best Friend Award for Boris from Amos. On the award, write why Boris is a good friend. Use details from the story.

Best Friend

To: Boris

From: Amos

Name ______________________________ Date ________

Boris's Speech

Boris is going to give a speech at the Meeting of the Whales about his adventures with Amos. Use the text and illustrations to answer questions about the events. Then, use your answers to write the speech.

Read page 13. How did Boris first meet Amos?

____

____

What did Boris first think about Amos when he saw him?

____

____

Read page 14. Where did Boris first want to take Amos?

____

____

How did Amos feel about this?

____

____

Name ______________________ Date ________

Read page 15.
What did Boris decide to do with Amos next?

____

____

Read pages 16–17.
What made Amos angry?

____

____

How did Amos and Boris solve this problem?

____

____

Read pages 18–19.

What happened over the next week?

____

____

____

Read page 20.

What happened on the last day that Boris and Amos were together?

____

____

____

Read page 21.

What happened after Boris left Amos at his home?

____

____

____

Name ______________________________ Date ________

Now use your answers to write Boris's speech. The speech should describe the events from Boris's point of view.

Speech for the Meeting of Whales

Name ______________________ Date ______

Amos and Boris

Interview with the Elephants

Imagine you are one of the elephants from the story and you are being interviewed for a radio program about Boris's rescue.

Read pages 22–23.
Tell me, Elephant, how did it all start?

____

____

Read page 24.
What happened when Amos, the mouse, came down to the beach?

____

____

What do you think it was like when Amos and Boris first saw each other again?

____

____

Read page 25. How do you think Boris felt when he saw Amos run off like that?

____

____

Read pages 26–28. That is where you come into the story. What did Amos say when he ran up to you?

____

____

How did you feel when you first saw Boris lying there on the beach?

____

____

What did you and your friend decide to do to help Boris?

____

____

____

____

Name ______________________________ Date ______

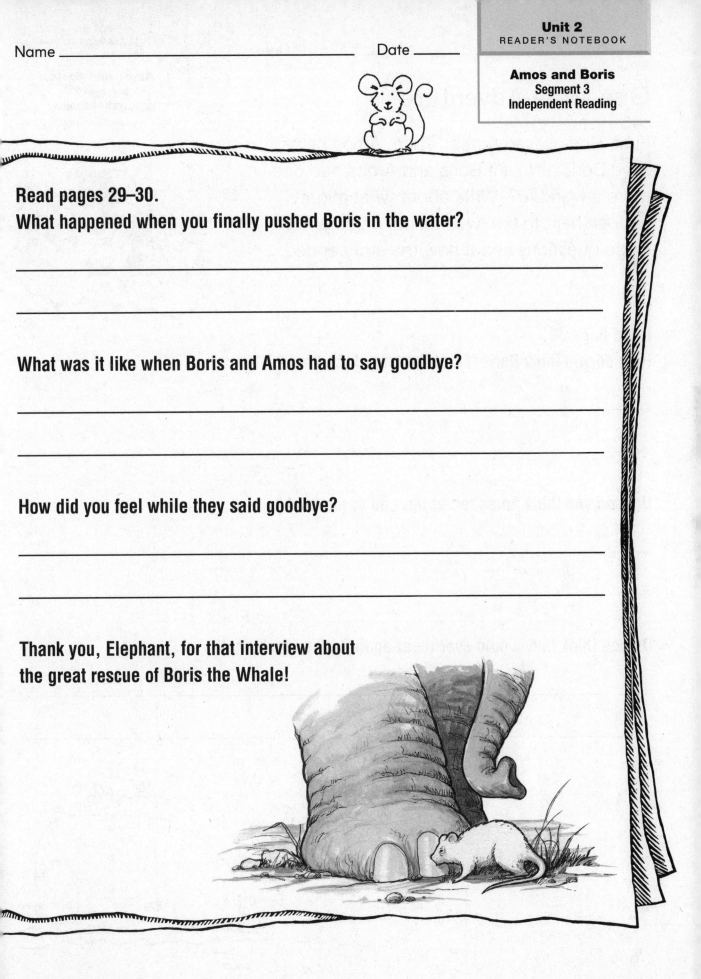

Read pages 29–30.
What happened when you finally pushed Boris in the water?

____

____

What was it like when Boris and Amos had to say goodbye?

____

____

How did you feel while they said goodbye?

____

____

Thank you, Elephant, for that interview about the great rescue of Boris the Whale!

Name ______________________________ Date ______

One More Adventure

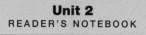

First, Boris saved Amos. Then, Amos helped save Boris. What if Boris and Amos had one more adventure? Write about what might happen next to the two friends. First, answer these questions about how the story ended.

Read page 30.

How do you think Boris felt at the end of the book?

____

____

How do you think Amos felt at the end of the book?

____

____

Do you think they would ever meet again? Why or why not?

____

____

Name ________________________ Date ______

Now think of another adventure for Amos and Boris. Plan your story below.

Who are the characters in your story?

____

____

____

____

What is the setting?

____

____

____

____

What problem do the characters have? How do they solve it?

____

____

____

____

Name ______________________ Date ______

Write your Amos and Boris story.
Draw a picture to go with it.

Name ________________________ Date ____________

Technology Wins the Game

Phonics: Words with Vowel Diphthongs *oi, oy*

Words with Vowel Diphthongs *oi*, *oy*

Read each sentence. Choose the missing word from the box. Write the word. Then reread the complete sentence.

broiling	ointment	soy
coiled	oyster	disappoint
voyage	avoid	hoist

1. While hiking, Debra saw a snake ____________ up on the path.
2. Before you can go sailing, you have to ____________ the sails.
3. Steve made sure to get his mom a birthday card so that he would not ____________ her.
4. My bike has a flat tire because I could not ____________ the broken glass on the sidewalk.
5. Christine cooked the hotdogs by ____________ them.
6. My grandmother is making a ____________ around the world.
7. I don't like seafood, so I did not eat the ____________.
8. Gwen put some ____________ on her poison ivy rash.
9. My mom eats burgers that are made with ____________ instead of meat.

Name ______________________ Date ____________

Changing *y* to *i*

- Add *-s* or *-es* to most singular nouns to form **regular plural nouns.**
- If a noun ends with a consonant and *y*, change the *y* to *i*, and add *-es* to form the plural.

Singular:	*family*	*party*
Plural:	*families*	*parties*

Thinking Question
Does the noun end with a consonant and y?

Write the plural form of each singular noun in parentheses. Then write a new sentence using the plural form of the noun.

1. My teammates and I play basketball in many ____________. (city)

____

2. We once played against a team that had ____________ on their shirts. (pony)

____

3. Another team had two ____________ on their shirts. (butterfly)

____

4. The teams are not really ____________. (enemy)

____

5. I made ____________ of the photos I took of the games. (copy)

____

Name ______________________ Date ____________

Technology Wins the Game
Grammar:
More Plural Nouns

Irregular Plural Nouns

- The spelling of **irregular plural nouns** changes in a special way.

  The woman wanted to be as tall as the other women.

- The spelling of some nouns does not change when they are plural.

  That black sheep is as large as all the other sheep.

- The noun *woman* changes to *women* when it is plural.
- The noun *sheep* remains *sheep* when it is plural.

Thinking Questions
Does the noun add -s or -es to form a plural, or does it change its spelling? Does its spelling not change?

Write the plural form of the noun in parentheses to complete each sentence.

1. Tara grew up to be stronger than most other ______________. (woman)
2. She was taller than most of the other ______________ her age. (child)
3. As she grew, she could run faster than most ______________. (deer)
4. Every fall she ran through the ______________. (leaf)
5. She ran and won many races against ______________. (man)
6. She lived on a farm with ducks and ______________. (goose)

Name ______________________ Date ____________

Technology Wins the Game
Spelling: Vowel Sound in *joy*

Vowel Sound in *joy*

Write each Basic Word under the correct heading.

Vowel Sound in *joy* spelled *oi*	Vowel Sound in *joy* spelled *oy*

Challenge: Add the Challenge Words to your Word Sort.

Spelling Words

Basic

1. joy
2. point
3. voice
4. join
5. oil
6. coin
7. noise
8. spoil
9. toy
10. joint
11. boy
12. soil
13. choice
14. boil

Review

come
are

Challenge

poison
destroy

Name ______________________ Date __________

Focus Trait: Word Choice

Signal Words

Cause	Effect
Amy practiced every day	won race

Sentence: <u>Because</u> Amy practiced every day, she won the race.

Read each cause and effect. Use a signal word to fill in the blank.

Cause	Effect
1. bought new running shoes	Cal's feet don't hurt
2. skier gets lost	sensor sends information

Sentence:

1. Cal bought new running shoes ____________ his feet don't hurt.
2. ____________ a skier gets lost, a sensor sends information.

Cause	Effect
3. tennis racket lighter	player can hit ball harder
4. Jana runs on grass	sometimes slips when it rains
5. water is cold	Max wears bodysuit

Sentence:

3. ______________________________
4. ______________________________
5. ______________________________

Name ____________________ Date __________

Cumulative Review

Write a word from the box to complete each sentence. Then read the complete sentence.

royal	cowboy	pointy
enjoy	avoid	voyage
oiled	loyal	noisy

1. The men working outside my window were so ____________ that I could not fall asleep.
2. Theresa is a ____________ friend, so I know I can trust her.
3. Marc knew that his trip around the world would be the ____________ of a lifetime.
4. The metal lid was rusted shut because no one had ____________ it for years.
5. A king and a queen are ____________ rulers.
6. Victor is mad at me, so he is trying to ____________ talking to me.
7. If you ____________ funny movies, you will love this one!
8. Once I get some fake ____________ ears, my elf costume will be complete.
9. Randy loved taking horseback riding lessons because it made him feel like a ____________.

Name ______________________________ Date ________

Technology Wins the Game

Sports Equipment Instruction Manual

You are writing a step-by-step manual that tells how sports equipment is made using the latest technology. It also explains how technology has changed over the years. Use information from the text to write the manual.

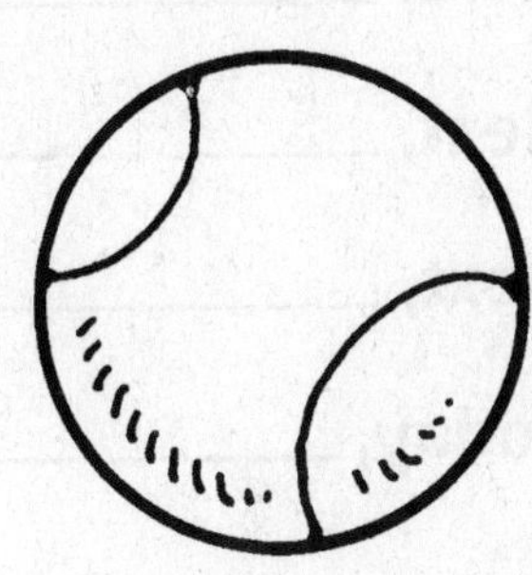

Read page 407. How are tennis balls made?

HOW TO MAKE A TENNIS BALL

Step 1: ______________________________

Step 2: ______________________________

Step 3: ______________________________

Step 4: ______________________________

Read page 408. How have vaulting poles changed over time?

THE HISTORY OF VAULTING POLES

First, ______________________________

Next, ______________________________

Then, ______________________________

Today, ______________________________

It took years to come up with the best technology for vaulting poles. But fiberglass is the best material because

____

Name ______________________ Date ________

Read page 410. How have running shoes changed over time? Use the text and the timeline to fill in the manual page.

THE HISTORY OF RUNNING SHOES

First, ______________________

Next, ______________________

Next, ______________________

Next, ______________________

Today, ______________________

____

Read page 412. How have football helmets changed over time?

THE HISTORY OF FOOTBALL HELMETS

First, ______________________

Next, ______________________

Then, ______________________

Next, ______________________

Next, ______________________

Today, ______________________

____

The newest technology for football helmets is computer chips. These help because ______________________

____

____

____

Name ______________________ Date ____________

Irregular Plural Nouns

Write the plural form of each singular noun in parentheses.

1. two tiny ______________ (baby)

2. four long ______________ (story)

3. twelve ripe ______________(cherry)

4. fresh red ______________ (berry)

5. eight cute ______________ (puppy)

Write *singular* or *plural* for each underlined noun.

6. Many women play sports. ______________

7. Many men take part in sports, too. ______________

8. Jack wore a guard to protect his teeth. ______________

9. A child can play sports at school. ______________

10. Geese do not play sports. ______________

Name ____________________ Date __________

Vowel Sound in *joy*

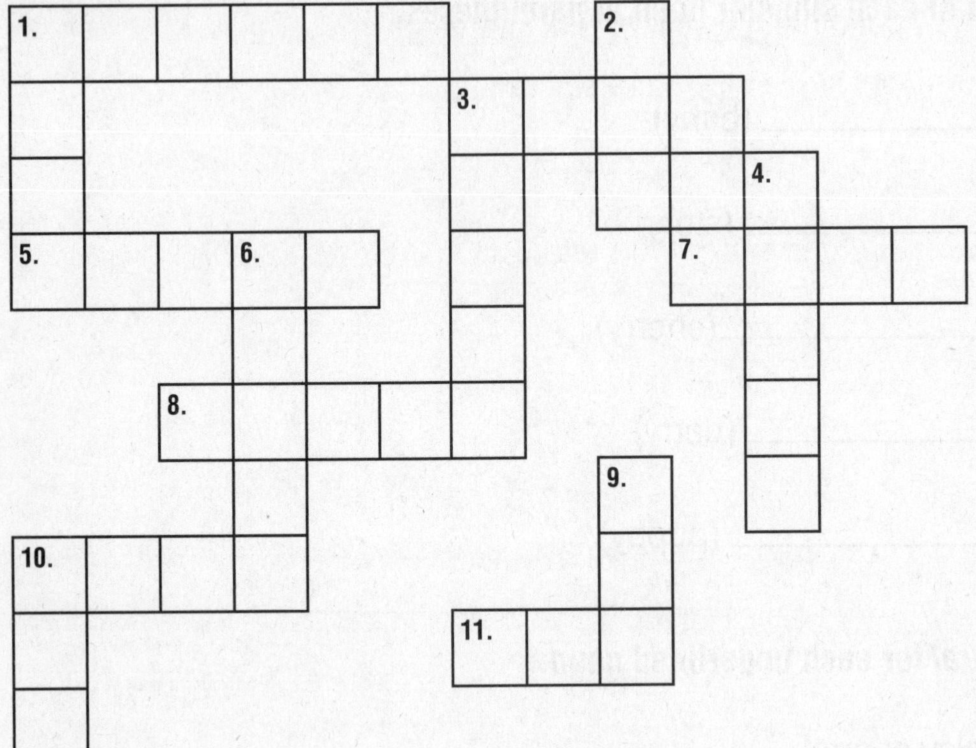

Spelling Words

Basic

1. joy
2. point
3. voice
4. join
5. oil
6. coin
7. noise
8. spoil
9. toy
10. joint
11. boy
12. soil
13. choice
14. boil

Review

come

are

Challenge

poison

destroy

Use the Basic Words to complete the puzzle.

Across

1. a decision

3. to become a member

5. a sound

7. dirt

8. the tip of a pencil

10. to heat a liquid until it bubbles

11. great happiness

Down

1. a metal piece of money

2. a dark, slippery liquid

3. the place where two bones connect

4. what one uses to speak

6. to go bad

9. something to play with

10. a male child

Name _______________ Date _______________

Technology Wins the Game
Vocabulary Strategies:
Suffixes *-less, -ful, -ous*

Suffixes *-less*, *-ful*, *-ous*

In each sentence, circle the word with the suffix *-less*, *-ful*, or *-ous*. Then write the base word, the suffix, and the word meaning. Use context clues in the sentence to help you find the meaning.

1. Uncle Mario is a skillful carpenter who can build just about anything out of wood.

   _______________ _______________ _______________
   base word **suffix** **meaning**

2. Gloria was happy to hear that her trip to the dentist would be painless.

   _______________ _______________ _______________
   base word **suffix** **meaning**

3. My grandmother is an adventurous person who likes to see new places and try new things.

   _______________ _______________ _______________
   base word **suffix** **meaning**

4. It is hard to say no to our coach because he is such a powerful person.

   _______________ _______________ _______________
   base word **suffix** **meaning**

5. Our dog Red sometimes yelps in his sleep, but he had a dreamless nap today.

   _______________ _______________ _______________
   base word **suffix** **meaning**

Kinds of Verbs

- A word that tells what people or things do is a **verb**. Words that show action are **action verbs**.
- Some verbs do not show action. They are **being verbs**. The verbs *am*, *is*, *are*, *was*, and *were* are forms of the verb *be*. They tell what someone or something is or was.

The players jump, and they are strong.

Identify the underlined verb in each sentence. Write *action* or *being* on the line.

1. Tammy worked hard for the race. ____________
2. She was a weak runner. ____________
3. Her coach taught her exercises. ____________

Combine each pair of sentences. Use both verbs in the new sentence. Write the new sentence on the line.

4. Jena jumped four feet high. Jena landed in the foam pit.

____

5. The team ran around the track. The team was soon tired.

____

6. The coaches were impressed. The coaches were happy.

____

Name ______________________ Date ____________

Technology Wins the Game
Spelling:
Vowel Sound in *joy*

Proofread for Spelling

Circle the ten misspelled Spelling Words in the following letter. Then write each word correctly.

Dear Louise,

I hope that you are doing well. I wish that I could jion you this week at camp. Sadly, I've lost my voic, so Mom says I have to rest. Sitting inside while everyone else has fun definitely wouldn't be my choyce. Boiy, am I bored! I did get a cool new toi, though. It is a tiny robot that makes a weird noyse whenever you poiynt a light at it. I think Dad wants to destroiy it already. He thinks playing with it is like poyson to my brain and says I should read more books. He's probably right. Oh, I also got a neat old coyn from my grandfather. Anyway, write back when you can!

Your friend,

Albert

Spelling Words

Basic

1. joy
2. point
3. voice
4. join
5. oil
6. coin
7. noise
8. spoil
9. toy
10. joint
11. boy
12. soil
13. choice
14. boil

Review

come
are

Challenge

poison
destroy

1. ______________ 6. ______________

2. ______________ 7. ______________

3. ______________ 8. ______________

4. ______________ 9. ______________

5. ______________ 10. ______________

Name ______________________ Date ____________

Connect to Writing

If a noun ends with a consonant and *y*, change the *y* to *i*, and add *-es* to form the plural.

Sometimes the spelling of a noun changes in a special way.

The spelling of some nouns does not change to form the plural.

Incorrectly Formed Plural	Correctly Formed Plural
cherry, cherrys	cherry, cherries
goose, gooses	goose, geese
deer, deers	deer, deer

Proofread the paragraph. Find five mistakes in the spelling of plural nouns. Write the corrected sentences on the lines below.

The mans on the ski team learned a lot from the women. They showed them how to relax and go faster. They told storys about great women skiers.

On top of the mountain, the skiers saw deers. They had to be careful not to run into them. Two women fell on the way down. Their familys were worried. But they were all right. Now they don't have any worrys.

1. ______________________
2. ______________________
3. ______________________
4. ______________________
5. ______________________

Name ______________________ Date ____________

Write Homophones

Read each sentence. Choose the missing word from the box. Write the word. Then reread the complete sentence.

chews	mail	heal
choose	cent	heel
male	sent	he'll

1. A stallion is a ______________ horse.
2. I didn't have a ______________ in my purse.
3. That wound should ______________ in a few days.
4. Becky's shoe was worn down at the ______________.
5. Ernesto always ______________ his food slowly.
6. Ginger's uncle ______________ her a birthday present.
7. Watch for an important letter in the ______________.
8. It is hard to ______________ between two of your favorite foods.
9. If the cat doesn't like his food, ______________ complain.

Name ____________________ Date ____________

Quotation Marks

Tops and Bottoms
Grammar:
Writing Quotations

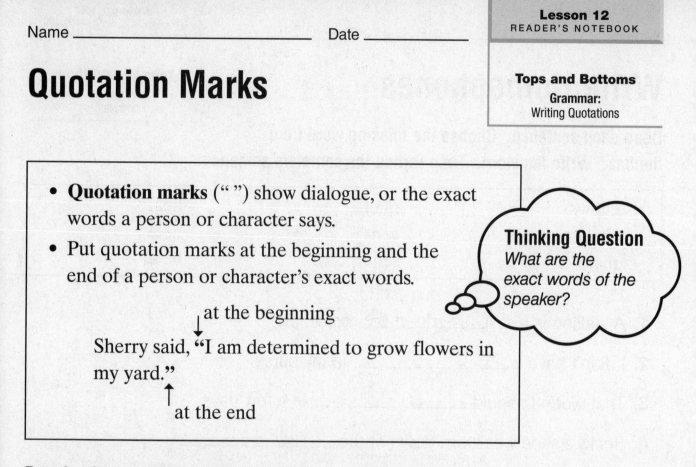

- **Quotation marks** (" ") show dialogue, or the exact words a person or character says.
- Put quotation marks at the beginning and the end of a person or character's exact words.

at the beginning ↓

Sherry said, **"**I am determined to grow flowers in my yard.**"**

↑ at the end

Thinking Question
What are the exact words of the speaker?

Rewrite the sentences, adding quotation marks as needed.

1. Sherry said, This summer, I will start a garden.

____

2. Cindy asked, What plants will you grow?

____

3. Sherry replied, I was thinking of planting sunflower seeds.

____

4. Cindy exclaimed, I love sunflowers!

____

Name ______________________ Date __________

Capitalizing and Punctuating Quotations

- Always capitalize the first word of the speaker's exact words.
- If the quotation comes first, add a comma, question mark, or exclamation point inside the **quotation marks** at the end of the speaker's words and add a period at the end of the sentence.
- If the quotation comes last, add a comma at the end of the tag and a question mark, exclamation point, or period inside the quotation marks.

Thinking Questions
What are the first and last words of the speaker? Which end mark is correct for the quotation? Does the quotation begin or end the sentence?

Rewrite the sentences with correct capitalization and punctuation.

1. Sherry exclaimed "my flowers are growing so well"

   ____

2. Marco asked "what did you do to help them grow"

   ____

3. "my sister and I weeded and watered them every day" replied Sherry

   ____

   ____

4. "carrying water is hard work" exclaimed Sherry

   ____

Name ________________________ Date ____________

Homophones

Write Basic Words to answer the following questions.

1. Which two words use the same vowel sound as *air?*

   ____________, ____________

2. Which two words use the same vowel sound as *ear?*

   ____________, ____________

3. Which two words use the same vowel sound as *burn?*

   ____________, ____________

4. Which two words use the same vowel sound as *once?*

   ____________, ____________

5. Which two words use the same vowel sound as *go?*

   ____________, ____________

6. Which two words use the same vowel sound as *in?*

   ____________, ____________

7. Which two words use the same vowel sound as *now?*

   ____________, ____________

Challenge: Write two sentences. Use one Challenge Word in each sentence.

1. ____

2. ____

Spelling Words

Basic

1. hole
2. whole
3. its
4. it's
5. hear
6. here
7. won
8. one
9. our
10. hour
11. their
12. there
13. fur
14. fir

Review

road
rode

Challenge

peace
piece

Name ______________________ Date ____________

Focus Trait: Word Choice

Signal Words

A compare-and-contrast paragraph tells how two or more things are alike and different. Good writers use signal words to help them compare and contrast things.

Without Signal Words: Carrots are orange. Lettuce is green.

With Signal Words: Carrots are orange, but lettuce is green.

Signal Words					
either	both	too	although	yet	however
or	but	and	neither	alike	different

Describe each vegetable.

Carrot	Beet
1.	
2.	

Write one sentence comparing and contrasting the vegetables.

3. ______________________________

4. ______________________________

Pair/Share Work with a partner to describe each vegetable. Then write a sentence comparing them and a sentence contrasting them.

Lettuce	Corn
5.	
6.	

7. ______________________________

8. ______________________________

Name ______________________ Date ____________

Words Ending in *-er, -le*

Write a word from the box to complete each sentence in the story. Then read the complete sentence.

bottle	ladle	table
dreamer	longer	teacher
kettle	sweeter	warmer

1. "Wake up, ______________!" my mom calls every morning.
2. "Can't I sleep a little ______________?" I always ask.
3. Soon I am in the kitchen, where it is ______________ and full of action.
4. The ______________ is already set for breakfast.
5. I get the ______________ of milk from the refrigerator.
6. In a few minutes the tea ______________ whistles and the water is ready.
7. I love making Mom's tea for her. "Just a bit more honey, to make it ______________," I say.
8. Then I watch as Dad puts a ______________ full of oatmeal in my favorite bowl. Yum!
9. He wraps up a muffin, smiles, and winks. "Give this to your ______________ before school today."

Name ______________________ Date ______

Tops and Bottoms

Gardening Journal

Hi, I'm Hare! I am keeping a garden journal to record the planting and harvesting. Help me fill it in with information from the text.

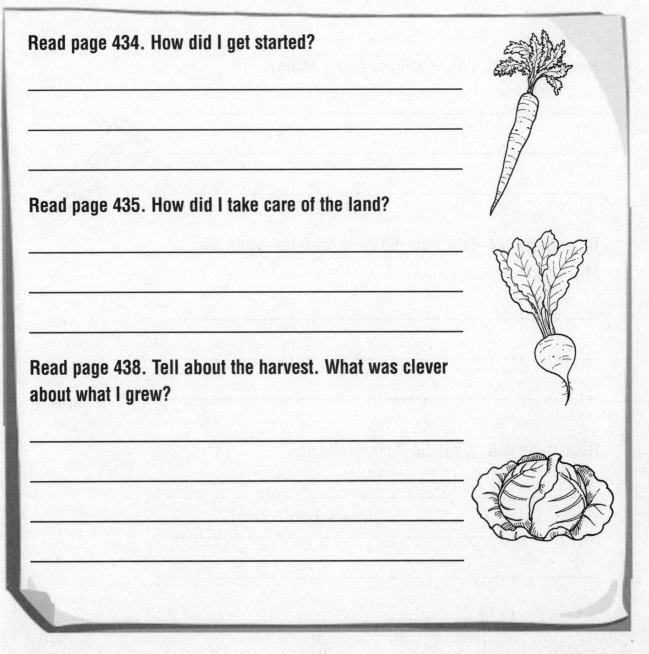

Read page 434. How did I get started?

____

____

____

Read page 435. How did I take care of the land?

____

____

____

Read page 438. Tell about the harvest. What was clever about what I grew?

____

____

____

____

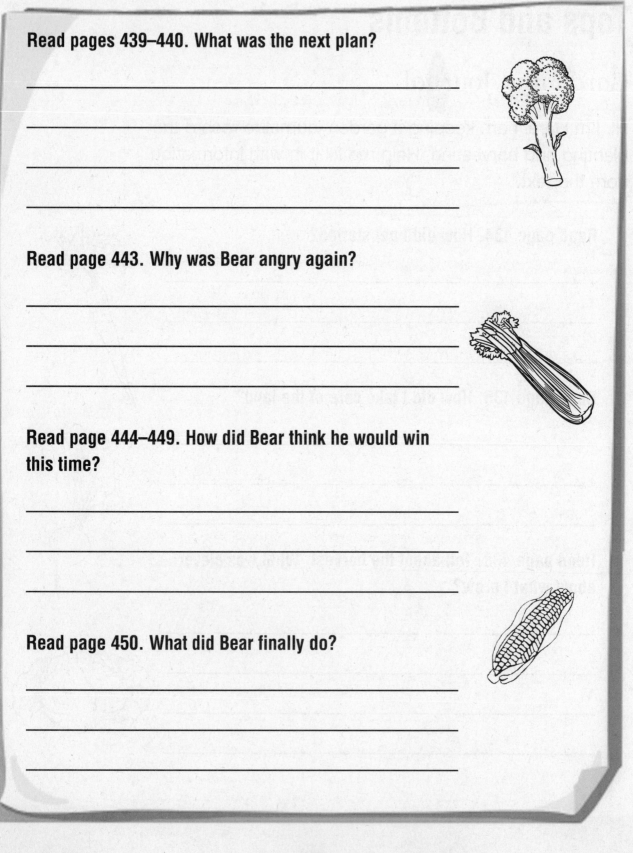

Read pages 439–440. What was the next plan?

Read page 443. Why was Bear angry again?

Read page 444–449. How did Bear think he would win this time?

Read page 450. What did Bear finally do?

Name ______________________ Date ____________

Capitalizing and Punctuating Quotations

- Capitalize the first word of the speaker's exact words.
- If the quotation comes first, add a comma, question mark, or exclamation point inside the **quotation marks** at the end of the speaker's words and add a period at the end of the sentence.
- If the quotation comes last, add a comma at the end of the tag and a question mark, exclamation point, or period inside the quotation marks.

Write the sentences using correct capitalization and punctuation.

1. Jessie asked "where are they selling their tomatoes"

____

2. "They have a roadside stand" replied Manny.

____

3. "Do they also sell cucumbers" asked Jessie.

____

4. "I'm not sure" Manny said.

____

5. Manny said "the stand is past this farm"

____

6. "They do have cucumbers" Jessie exclaimed.

____

Name ______________________ Date ______________

Who Am I?

Read each clue. Then write the correct word on the line.

1. Every day has 24 of me. ______________
2. Wolves and bears wear me. ______________
3. If you fall into me you might get hurt.

   ____
4. I am all, not just part. ______________
5. I am first! ______________
6. I have needles instead of leaves. ______________
7. I am something people do with their ears.

   ____
8. I am something a team did. ______________

Challenge: Explain the meanings of *peace* and *piece*.

____

____

Spelling Words

Basic

1. hole
2. whole
3. its
4. it's
5. hear
6. here
7. won
8. one
9. our
10. hour
11. their
12. there
13. fur
14. fir

Review

road

rode

Challenge

peace

piece

Name ______________________ Date ____________

Idioms

Tops and Bottoms
Vocabulary Strategies:
Idioms

Read the web below. Write the meaning of each idiom. (You may find the meanings by looking up *head* in the dictionary.)

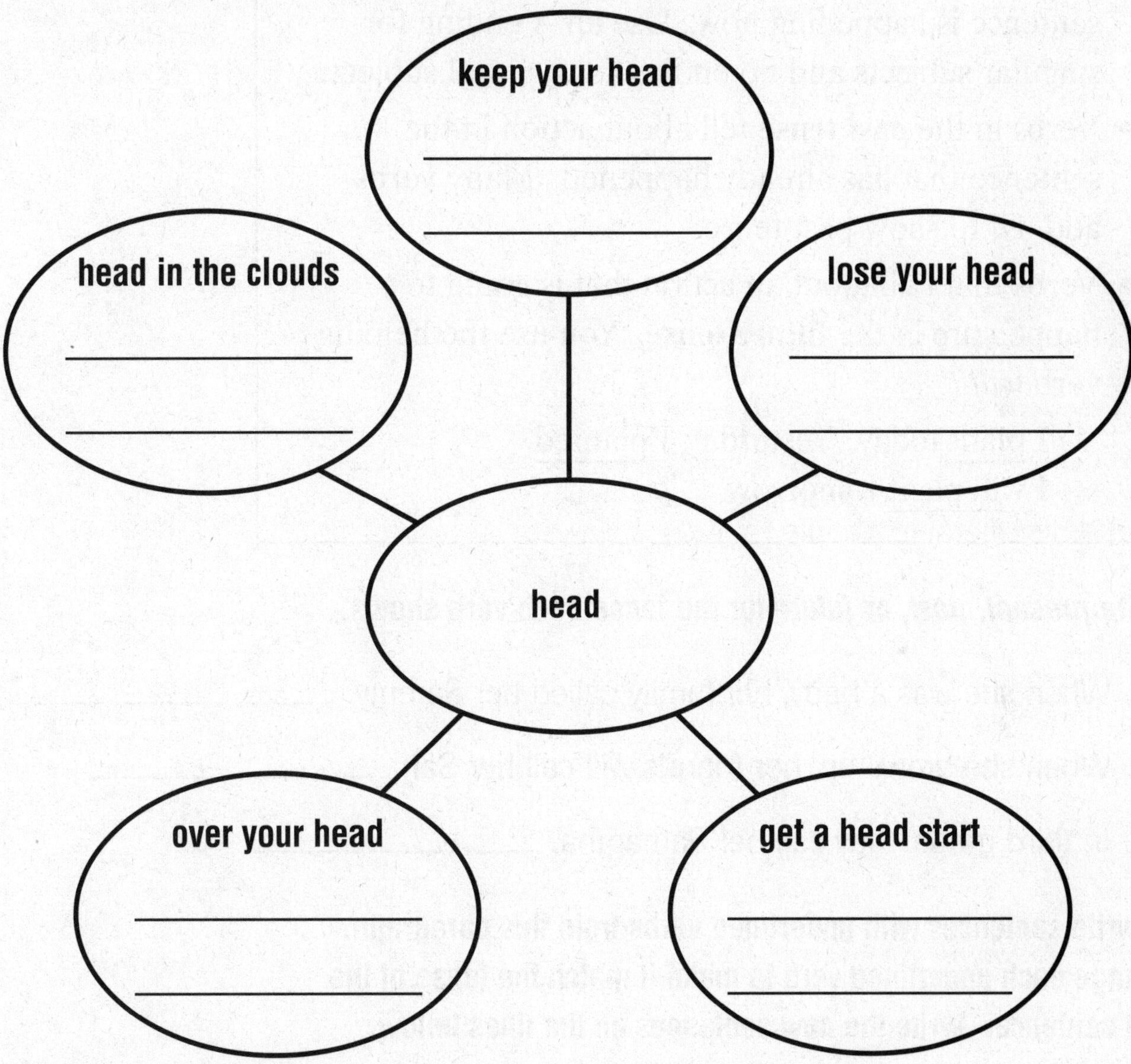

Choose one idiom from above and write two sentences. In the first sentence, write the meaning of the idiom. In the second sentence, replace the meaning with the idiom.

1. ____

2. ____

Name _______________ Date _______________

Verb Tenses

- Verbs in the **present tense** tell that the action in the sentence is happening now. Use an *-s* ending for singular subjects and no ending for a plural subject.
- Verbs in the **past tense** tell about action in the sentence that has already happened. Many verbs add *-ed* to show past tense.
- Verbs that tell about an action that is going to happen are in the **future tense**. You use the helping verb *will*.

  I plant today. Yesterday, I planted.
  I will plant tomorrow.

Write *present*, *past*, or *future* for the tense each verb shows.

1. When she was a baby, her family called her Sammy. _______________
2. When she grows up, her friends will call her Sam. _______________
3. In third grade, they call her Samantha. _______________

Rewrite sentences with underlined verbs from this paragraph. Change each underlined verb to make it match the tense of the first sentence. Write the new sentences on the lines below.

Our dog, Yappy, ran into the street. My brother calls to him very loudly. Yappy will stop for my brother.

4. ____

5. ____

Name ______________________ Date __________

Tops and Bottoms
Spelling:
Homophones

Proofreading for Spelling

Find the misspelled words and circle them. Then write each word correctly.

Dear Pat,

I'm writing this in the shade of a big fur tree. Its soft needles cover the ground like a blanket. Its a quiet summer day in the city's biggest park. All around, their is a feeling of piece and restfulness. My dog, Corvo, lies lazily in the hot sun. I'll bet his fir makes him hot on this summer day. I pick up a peace of paper that someone has left on the ground. Let's keep the city clean! I've been hear an our, and I could stay all day. I can hardly here the traffic. The cars with there noise seem far away. I like writing letters, but I wish you were here!

Your friend,
Chris

Spelling Words

Basic

1. hole
2. whole
3. its
4. it's
5. hear
6. here
7. won
8. one
9. our
10. hour
11. their
12. there
13. fur
14. fir

Review

road
rode

Challenge

peace
piece

1. ______________ 6. ______________
2. ______________ 7. ______________
3. ______________ 8. ______________
4. ______________ 9. ______________
5. ______________ 10. ______________

Name ______________________ Date ____________

Connect to Writing

Use quotation marks (“ ”) to show the exact words someone says. A quotation may come before or after the tag.

Before the Tag	After the Tag
“I'll help make dinner,” Ralph said.	Ralph said, “I'll help make dinner.”
“What would you like to eat?” Pete asked.	Pete asked, “What would you like to eat?”

Rewrite the sentences, adding quotation marks and commas as needed.

1. I would like roasted vegetables Ralph replied.

____

2. Pete said I have carrots.

____

3. Would you like carrots Pete asked.

____

4. I love carrots! Ralph exclaimed.

____

5. They are one of my favorites said Pete.

____

Name ______________________ Date ____________

Contractions with *n't*, *'d*, *'ve*

Yonder Mountain: A Cherokee Legend
Phonics: Contractions with *n't*, *'d*, *'ve*

Read each sentence. Choose the missing word from the box. Write the word. Then reread the complete sentence.

aren't	couldn't	should've
they'd	you'd	haven't
I've	we've	I'd

1. If I ever had to sleep in the woods, ______________ bring lots of bug spray.
2. I tried to open the jar, but I ______________ because the lid was on too tight.
3. If you saw the movie, ______________ love it as much as I did.
4. My parents ______________ too strict, but they do have some rules.
5. Personally, ______________ always admired Ben Franklin.
6. We haven't seen the movie, but ______________ both read the book.
7. "I ______________ known that you were behind all of this," said the hero to the villain.
8. Why are you serving us dessert when we ______________ eaten dinner yet?
9. If our friends saw us, ______________ be really surprised.

Name _______________________ Date ___________

Subject-Verb Agreement

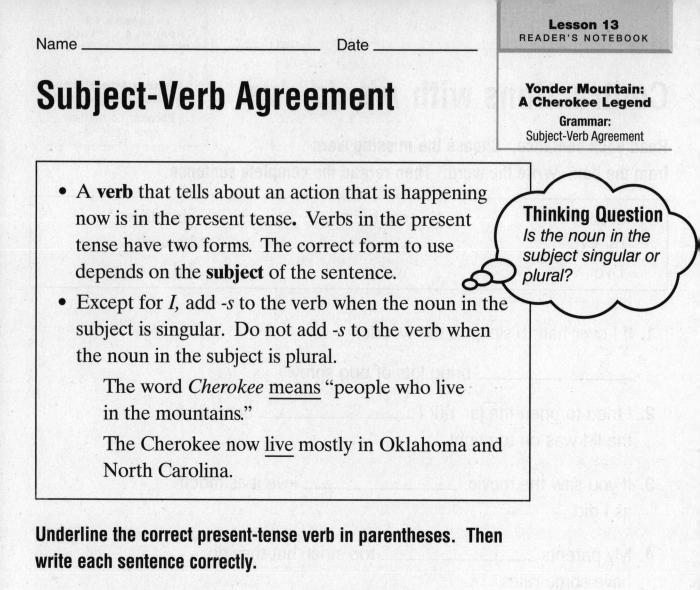

- A **verb** that tells about an action that is happening now is in the present tense**.** Verbs in the present tense have two forms. The correct form to use depends on the **subject** of the sentence.
- Except for *I,* add *-s* to the verb when the noun in the subject is singular. Do not add *-s* to the verb when the noun in the subject is plural.

  The word *Cherokee* means "people who live in the mountains."

  The Cherokee now live mostly in Oklahoma and North Carolina.

Thinking Question
Is the noun in the subject singular or plural?

Underline the correct present-tense verb in parentheses. Then write each sentence correctly.

1. People (hear, hears) the Cherokee language.

   ____

2. Fur trader Abraham Wood (send, sends) two men.

   ____

3. The program about the Cherokee (begins, begin) at 7:00.

   ____

4. The Cherokee (moves, move) to the west in the 1880s.

   ____

Name ______________________________ Date ____________

Yonder Mountain: A Cherokee Legend
Grammar:
Subject-Verb Agreement

Subject-Verb Agreement

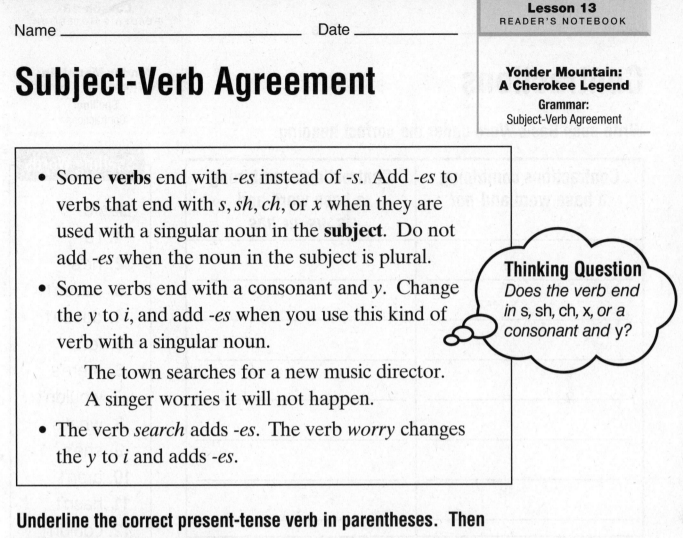

- Some **verbs** end with *-es* instead of *-s*. Add *-es* to verbs that end with *s*, *sh*, *ch*, or *x* when they are used with a singular noun in the **subject**. Do not add *-es* when the noun in the subject is plural.
- Some verbs end with a consonant and *y*. Change the *y* to *i*, and add *-es* when you use this kind of verb with a singular noun.

  The town searches for a new music director.
  A singer worries it will not happen.

- The verb *search* adds *-es*. The verb *worry* changes the *y* to *i* and adds *-es*.

Thinking Question
Does the verb end in s, sh, ch, x, *or a consonant and* y*?*

Underline the correct present-tense verb in parentheses. Then write each sentence correctly.

1. A newspaper writer (asks, askes) for a new music director.

____

2. A town citizen (watchs, watches) for a new music director.

____

3. A woman who knows music (hurrys, hurries) into town.

____

4. She (trys, tries) to get everyone to sing well together.

____

Name ______________________ Date ____________

Yonder Mountain: A Cherokee Legend
Spelling:
Contractions

Contractions

Write each Basic Word under the correct heading.

Contractions combining a base word and *not*	Contractions combining a base word and *is*, *us*, or *has*
______________	______________
______________	______________
______________	______________
______________	______________
______________	______________
______________	______________
______________	______________

Contractions combining a base word and *are*	Contractions combining a base word and *had* or *would*
______________	______________
______________	______________
______________	______________

Challenge: Add the Challenge Words to your Word Sort.

Spelling Words

Basic

1. I'd
2. he's
3. haven't
4. doesn't
5. let's
6. there's
7. wouldn't
8. what's
9. she's
10. aren't
11. hasn't
12. couldn't
13. he'd
14. they're

Review

can't
isn't

Challenge

we're
weren't

Name ______________________ Date ______________

Focus Trait: Organization

Group Related Information

An informative paragraph gives facts and details about a topic. When you write an informative paragraph, group related information together.

Read pages 479–480 of *Yonder Mountain*. Write facts and details about Gray Wolf in the web.

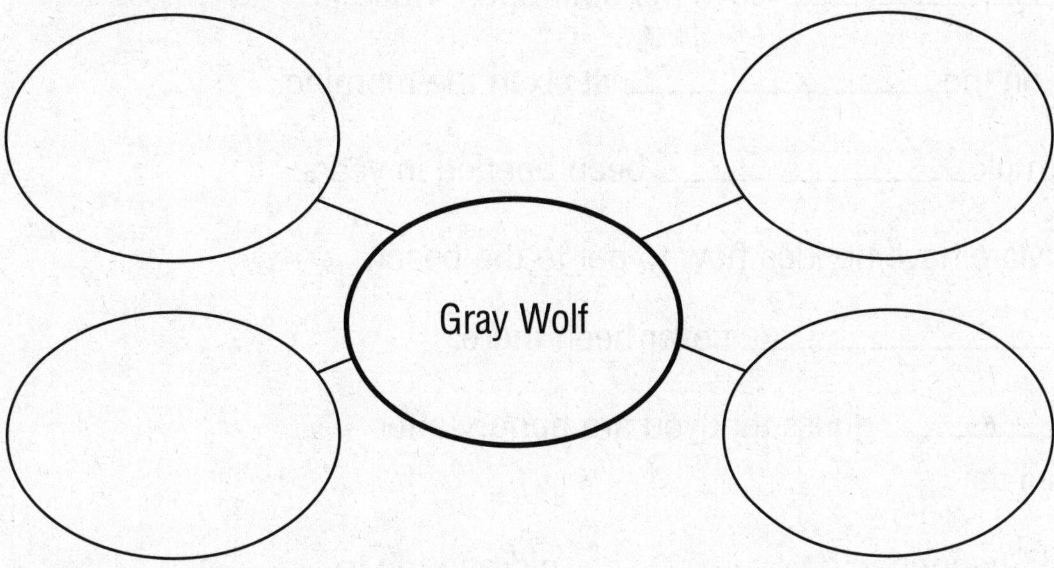

Pair/Share **Work with a partner to write sentences that group the information in the web.**

____

____

____

____

____

Name _______________ Date _______________

Cumulative Review

Write a word from the box to complete each sentence. Then read the sentence.

road	they've	we've
you'd	I'd	rode
aren't	hasn't	didn't

1. If you _______________ leave the door open, who did?
2. We were on the _______________ at six in the morning.
3. This old trunk _______________ been opened in years.
4. Eric and Marc have no idea how to get to the beach because _______________ never been there.
5. _______________ guess that you are hungry after working all day.
6. Carla and Shannon _______________ old enough to stay up so late.
7. Dee was excited to tell her friends how she _______________ a horse on vacation.
8. If _______________ just listen more, and talk less, you could learn a lot.
9. My cousin pulled me outside, saying, "_______________ got to leave now!"

Name ______________________________ Date ________

Yonder Mountain

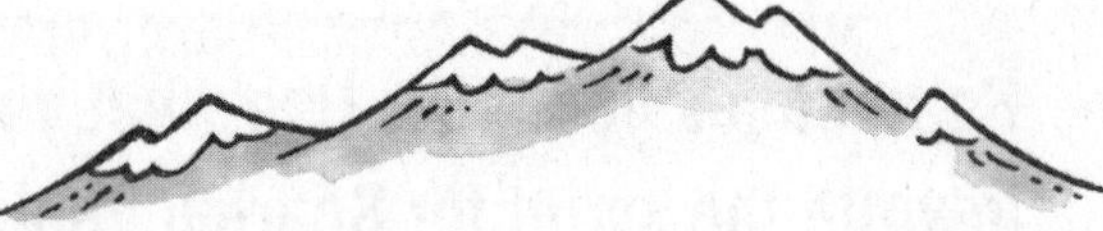

A Scene from Yonder Mountain

You are going to tell the story of Yonder Mountain as a play. Fill in the different parts with details from the story.

Read pages 473–475. Use what you read on these pages to write a script for Chief Sky. Help him tell the audience how the three young men are alike. What do they want? What do they do?

Chief Sky: ______________________________

____

____

Read pages 476–480. Use these pages to help Black Bear and Gray Wolf tell the audience about their adventures.

Black Bear: ______________________________

____

____

Gray Wolf: ______________________________

____

____

Read pages 481–484. Use what you read on these pages to write the script for Soaring Eagle. He will tell the audience about his journey up the mountain.

Soaring Eagle: ______________________________

____

____

____

____

Read pages 485–487. Why did Chief Sky choose Soaring Eagle to be the new chief? Write a script for Chief Sky. He will tell the audience why he chose Soaring Eagle.

Chief Sky: ______________________________

____

____

____

____

Name ______________________ Date ____________

Subject-Verb Agreement

The subject of each sentence is underlined. Write the correct form of the verb in parentheses to complete each sentence.

1. A climber ______________ for a way to the top. (search)
2. Two strong men ______________ themselves up the cliffs. (pull)
3. A woman ______________ her ropes to be safe. (fix)
4. One person ______________ another as they climb. (pass)
5. Friends ______________ someone who is tired. (help)
6. Some boys ______________ to see who can be first to the top. (race)
7. A bird ______________ up to the highest point. (fly)
8. One group ______________ a deep valley on the way. (cross)
9. One tired person ______________ on the way up. (slip)
10. I ______________ the top of the mountain first. (reach)

Name ______________________ Date ____________

Yonder Mountain: A Cherokee Legend
Spelling: Contractions

Contractions

Write the Spelling Word that is a contraction of each word pair below.

1. have not ____________
2. what is ____________
3. let us ____________
4. he had ____________
5. could not ____________
6. there is ____________
7. are not ____________
8. she is ____________
9. they are ____________
10. does not ____________
11. I had ____________
12. would not ____________
13. he is ____________
14. has not ____________

Spelling Words

Basic

1. I'd
2. he's
3. haven't
4. doesn't
5. let's
6. there's
7. wouldn't
8. what's
9. she's
10. aren't
11. hasn't
12. couldn't
13. he'd
14. they're

Review

can't
isn't

Challenge

we're
weren't

Name ______________________ Date __________

Homophones and Homographs

Yonder Mountain

Vocabulary Strategies:
Homophones and Homographs

Read the following paragraph. Proofread it to find mistakes with homophones. Write the wrong homophone and the correct homophone on the lines.

My grandmother and I walked to the park. On our weigh, we passed a fruit stand.

"Mind if we peak at your selection?" my grandmother asked.

"Go ahead!" the fruit vendor said. "I have all kinds of fresh fruits write here! Here, have this red pare," he added. "It's perfectly ripe."

"Thanks," my grandmother said. "I almost mist that one!"

1. ______________________
2. ______________________
3. ______________________
4. ______________________
5. ______________________

Choose a pair of homophones. Write a sentence that shows the meaning of each word.

____

____

Name ____________________ Date ____________

Writing Quotations

- Show dialogue by putting quotation marks (" ") at the beginning and the end of a speaker's exact words.

  She asked, "Are you climbing?"

- Place a comma after *said* or *asked.* Use a capital letter for the first word of the quotation and an end mark inside the quotation marks.

  He said, "Give it to me."

  "We're finally home!" Kim shouted.

Write each sentence correctly by adding quotation marks.

1. The teacher said, Hillary climbed the tallest mountain.

____

2. She asked, What is the tallest mountain called?

____

3. He said, It is named Mount Everest.

____

Write each sentence correctly. Use quotation marks, correct capitalization, end marks, and punctuation.

4. The teacher asked would you like to climb a mountain

____

5. The girl said climbing Mount Everest would be exciting

____

Name ______________________ Date __________

Yonder Mountain: A Cherokee Legend
Spelling: Contractions

Proofreading

Circle the ten misspelled Spelling Words in the following story. Then write each word correctly.

My Relatives

My aunt and uncle are very different from a lot of people. Hes a clown in a circus, and she works as a stuntwoman. Theyr'e always doing crazy stuff. For example, my aunt has'nt cut her hair in fifteen years. I know I couln'ot go six months without getting a haircut. Then theres the house where they live. Lets' just say that it is unique. For starters, it do'snt have any corners. You wouldnt believe how odd it looks. When we stay with them, I feel like wer'e living in a donut! If they were'nt so nice, I might think that there was actually something wrong with them.

1. ______________
2. ______________
3. ______________
4. ______________
5. ______________
6. ______________
7. ______________
8. ______________
9. ______________
10. ______________

Spelling Words

Basic

1. I'd
2. he's
3. haven't
4. doesn't
5. let's
6. there's
7. wouldn't
8. what's
9. she's
10. aren't
11. hasn't
12. couldn't
13. he'd
14. they're

Review

can't
isn't

Challenge

we're
weren't

Name ______________________ Date ____________

Connect to Writing

Proofreading is important to make writing correct and clear to the reader. Pay attention to endings of verbs as you proofread.

Singular Subject	Plural Subject
The Native American chief leads.	Chiefs lead.
He mixes an herb as medicine.	They mix herbs as medicine.
The chief thinks about his people.	Chiefs think about their people.
He works for a solution.	They work for a solution.

Proofread the paragraph. Find and underline five errors with the spelling of present tense verbs. Write the corrected sentences.

The chief of the Native American group knows it is time to move. The land lack the food needed for their people. It is time to go south. The women carries the things they want to bring. Some men on horses searches for a place to stay. They find a wonderful place by the river. The children rushes to get there first. Everyone enjoys the new area. A horse splash through the river water. Everyone smiles for the first time in a long time.

1. ______________________________

2. ______________________________

3. ______________________________

4. ______________________________

5. ______________________________

Name ______________________ Date ____________

Words with *ar, or, ore*

Read each sentence. Choose the missing word from the box. Write the word. Then reread the sentence.

Mars	morning	cart
chores	parking	largest
artistic	explore	parlor

1. This tree is the ______________ tree on the street.
2. "Have a seat in the ______________," said the butler to the guest.
3. The bold scientists planned to ______________ the bottom of the ocean.
4. The driver looked for a ______________ space for five minutes.
5. Put your groceries into the ______________.
6. My favorite time of day is ______________.
7. Painting, singing, and dancing are ______________ hobbies.
8. I wish I could fly to the planet ______________.
9. Taking out the trash and making my bed are on my list of ______________.

Name ______________________ Date ____________

Pronoun-Verb Agreement

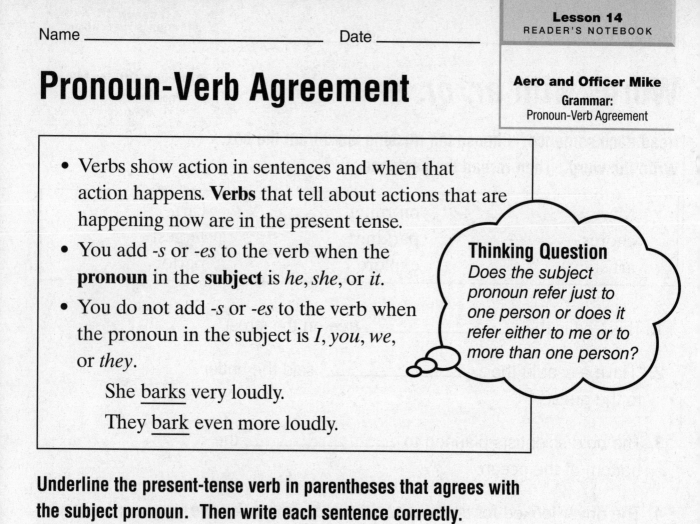

- Verbs show action in sentences and when that action happens. **Verbs** that tell about actions that are happening now are in the present tense.
- You add *-s* or *-es* to the verb when the **pronoun** in the **subject** is *he*, *she*, or *it*.
- You do not add *-s* or *-es* to the verb when the pronoun in the subject is *I*, *you*, *we*, or *they*.

She barks very loudly.

They bark even more loudly.

Thinking Question
Does the subject pronoun refer just to one person or does it refer either to me or to more than one person?

Underline the present-tense verb in parentheses that agrees with the subject pronoun. Then write each sentence correctly.

1. You (find, finds) dogs of all different types.

____

2. He (choose, chooses) the ones that are the best.

____

3. It (seem, seems) that you know dogs well.

____

4. We (feel, feels) that you should choose the dogs.

____

5. They (want, wants) to pick out some dogs, too.

____

Name ____________________ Date __________

When to Add *-es*, *-ies*

- Most **verbs** in the present end with *-s* when the **pronoun** in the **subject** is *he*, *she*, or *it*. Add *-es* to verbs that end in *-s*, *-sh*, *-ch*, or *-x*.
- Do not add *-s* or *-es* to verbs when the pronoun in the subject is *I*, *you*, *we*, or *they*.
- Some verbs end with a consonant and *y*. Change the *y* to *i* and add *-es* when the pronoun in the subject is *he*, *she*, or *it*.
- You do not change the *y* to *i* and add *-es* when the pronoun in the subject is *I*, *you*, *we*, or *they*.

Thinking Question
Does the verb end in s, sh, ch, x *or with a consonant and* y, *and what is the pronoun in the subject?*

Underline the present-tense verb in parentheses that agrees with the subject pronoun. Then write each sentence correctly.

1. You (push, pushes) the cart filled with hay out to the fields.

____

2. It (pass, passes) over the old bridge.

____

3. We (guess, guesses) when you will reach the horses.

____

4. They (march, marches) across the hills to the food.

____

Name ____________________ Date ____________

Words with Vowel + /r/ Sounds

Write the correct Basic Words in each box.

Write the words that contain the vowel + *r* sound in *far*.	Write the words that contain the vowel + *r* sound in *or*.
____________	____________
____________	____________
____________	____________
____________	____________
____________	____________
	____________
	____________
	____________
	____________

Spelling Words

Basic

1. horse
2. mark
3. storm
4. market
5. acorn
6. artist
7. March
8. north
9. barking
10. stork
11. thorn
12. forest
13. chore
14. restore

Review

dark
story

Challenge

partner
fortune

Challenge

1. Does *partner* contain the vowel sound in *far* or the vowel sound in *or*? ____________
2. Does *fortune* contain the vowel sound in *far* or the vowel sound in *or*? ____________

Name ______________________ Date ____________

Focus Trait: Ideas

Choosing a Topic

An explanatory essay uses ideas, facts, and details to explain a topic to readers. Good writers ask, *What topic am I interested in? What ideas do I have about the topic? How can I use facts and details to explain the topic clearly?*

Read the information in the chart. Look at the topics and the author's purpose. Which topic interests you the most? Circle it.

Topics	Author's Purpose
how dogs help people how monkeys help people how horses help people how dolphins help people	To explain a topic to readers

Tell why you chose the topic. Also list one or two ideas that you have about the topic.

____

____

____

____

Name ______________________ Date ____________

Cumulative Review

Write words from the box to complete the lines of the poem.

arm	garden	I'd	shark	storm
bored	harm	I've	shore	thorns

What Didn't Go Wrong Today?

I worked in my ________(1), but I soon came to ________(2).
The sharp ________(3) of a rose badly scratched up
my ________(4)!
So I went to the ________(5) for a swim and some sun,
Until a ________(6) showed its fin and scared everyone!
Then ________(7) just reached the woods, the shade of tall trees,
When a dark ________(8) filled the sky and rained on the seas!
Now ________(9) come home sad, with nothing to do.
If you are ________(10), too, may I come play with you?

Aero and Officer Mike

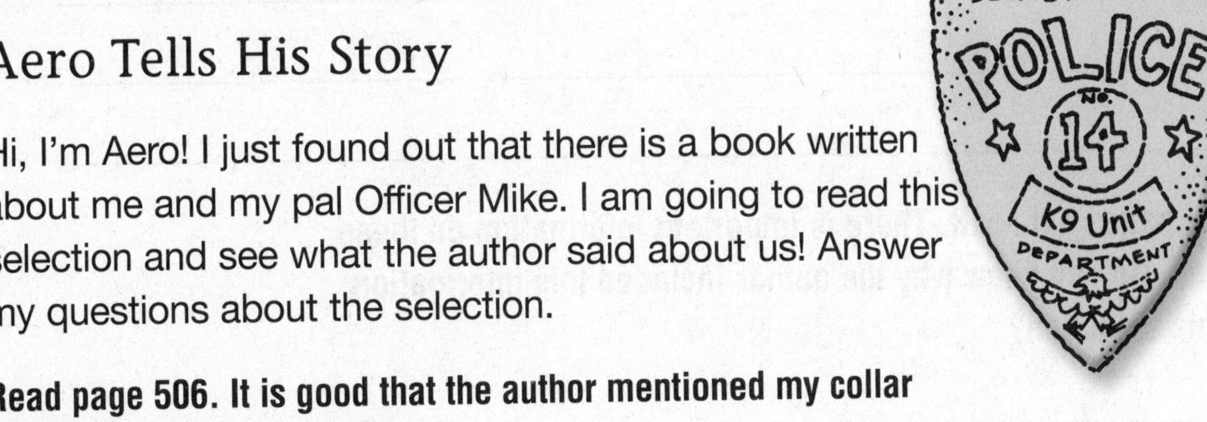

Aero Tells His Story

Hi, I'm Aero! I just found out that there is a book written about me and my pal Officer Mike. I am going to read this selection and see what the author said about us! Answer my questions about the selection.

Read page 506. It is good that the author mentioned my collar first thing! Do you know why?

____

____

Read pages 508–509. The author mentioned Officer Mike's police car. Why do you think the car is important?

____

____

____

Read pages 510–511. I love playing ball with Mike! I also listen to Mike when he talks to me. Can you guess why?

____

____

Name ______________________ Date ______

Read page 512. I remember that training! I still don't really like looking at those pictures. What can you tell about the training from looking at the pictures? How did I feel about it?

____

____

____

Read pages 516–518. There is important information on these pages. Do you know why the author included this information in this selection?

____

____

____

Read pages 519–521. I thought this was a really good book! It explained a lot about Officer Mike and me! Now you tell me what you thought of this selection. Did you like it? Why or why not?

____

____

____

Name ______________________ Date ____________

Pronoun-Verb Agreement

Write the present-tense form of the verb in parentheses that agrees with the subject pronoun.

1. My dogs ________________ all day. (sleep)

2. They ________________ my smell and trust me. (learn)

3. He ________________ other ways to get close to his dogs. (use)

4. She ________________ them right out of her hand. (feed)

5. You ________________ here and watch us do it. (sit)

6. The dogs ________________ as they play in the rain. (splash)

7. It ________________ your attention when you see it. (catch)

8. He ________________ a special blend of pet food. (mix)

9. One ________________ a ball that he throws. (catch)

10. They ________________ the different ways to train pets. (study)

Name ______________________ Date ____________

Words with Vowel + /r/ Sounds

Write eight words that are names for people, places, or things.

____

____

____

____

____

____

____

____

Challenge

1. A person you work with is your ______________.
2. If you make a lot of money, you make a ______________.

Spelling Words

Basic

1. horse
2. mark
3. storm
4. market
5. acorn
6. artist
7. March
8. north
9. barking
10. stork
11. thorn
12. forest
13. chore
14. restore

Review

dark
story

Challenge

partner
fortune

Name ______________________ Date ____________

Prefixes *in-*, *im-*

Read each base word. Add the prefix shown and write a new word and its meaning.

Base Word	Prefix	New Word	Meaning
active	in		
visible	in		
definite	in		
patient	im		
perfect	im		
measurable	im		

Now write a sentence for each word above with a prefix. Make sure your sentence shows the word's meaning.

1. ______________________________

2. ______________________________

3. ______________________________

4. ______________________________

5. ______________________________

6. ______________________________

Name ________________ Date ________

Subjects and Predicates

- The subject of a sentence tells whom or what the sentence is about.
- The predicate of a sentence tells what the subject is, was, or will be, or what the subject is, was, or will be doing.

  The sheep ate grass in the valley.

  An old wolf watched them from the bushes.

Write the subject of each sentence on the line.

1. The old gray coyote came out of the hills. ________
2. This smart animal will eat almost anything. ________
3. His little pups hide right behind him. ________
4. These sweet babies are hungry and tired. ________

Write the predicate of each sentence on the line.

5. Three fat sheep walk away from the others. ________
6. A big blue truck drives by them. ________
7. A man with boots grabs the sheep. ________
8. The coyote finds food for the pups. ________

Name ____________________ Date __________

Words with Vowel + /r/ Sounds

Aero and Officer Mike
Spelling:
Vowel + /r/ Sounds

Find the misspelled words and circle them. Then write each word correctly.

An ortist was traveling through a deep, dark farest. He carried his paints and brushes in a bag that hung from his back. His harse was white, just like a blank canvas. He was riding to the morket, a day's ride to the narth, to sell his pictures. Suddenly, huge gray clouds moved overhead. A storem was coming! The wind rose, and an acarn fell from a tree, hitting the man on the head. A sharp tharn from a bush scratched his hand. A big white stark flapped its wings as it flew toward its nest. Then the traveler heard the barrking of wild dogs in the distance. "Don't worry," he told his horse. "They're afraid of thunder and lightning."

1. ______________
2. ______________
3. ______________
4. ______________
5. ______________
6. ______________
7. ______________
8. ______________
9. ______________
10. ______________

Spelling Words

Basic

1. horse
2. mark
3. storm
4. market
5. acorn
6. artist
7. March
8. north
9. barking
10. stork
11. thorn
12. forest
13. chore
14. restore

Review

dark
story

Challenge

partner
fortune

Name ______________________ Date ____________

Connect to Writing

Combining two sentences that have the same noun in the subject makes your writing smoother and easier to read. Remember to use a comma and the word *and*.

Same Noun in the Subject	Pronoun Replacing Noun in the Subject
These dogs are for sports. These dogs make great pets.	These dogs are for sports, and they make great pets.
Border collies are herding dogs. Border collies are very smart.	Border collies are herding dogs, and they are very smart.

Combine each pair of sentences. Change each underlined subject to a pronoun. Write the new sentence.

1. Maltese dogs are friendly. Maltese dogs make good pets.

   ____

2. My male Great Dane is very gentle. My male Great Dane stands very tall.

   ____

3. Your female collie tends sheep. Your female collie gets burrs in her fur.

   ____

4. The people who breed dogs work very hard. The people who breed dogs love animals.

   ____

5. My family and I look for the perfect dog. My family and I find a funny one we love.

   ____

Name ______________________ Date ____________

Words with *er, ir, ur, or*

Read each sentence. Choose the missing word from the box. Write the word. Then reread the complete sentence.

curb	nerve	curves
worker	furry	birth
thirty	germs	

1. The road ______________ up ahead, so be ready to turn.
2. Having hair on the furniture is one of the problems with having a ______________ dog.
3. I knew you wouldn't have the ______________ to stand up to your big brother.
4. As Danielle crossed the street, she tripped on the ______________ and hurt her ankle.
5. Adam does well in school because he is a hard ______________.
6. The zoo announced the ______________ of a baby panther last week.
7. Mr. Perkins has ______________ students in his classroom.
8. Colds and the flu are caused by ______________.

Name ______________________ Date ____________

Verbs in the Past

- Most verbs show **past tense** by adding *-ed.*
- Some verbs end with *e.* Drop the *e* and add *-ed.*

They allowed us to cook alone.

He needed eggs for the recipe.

Evan's parents liked our cooking.

Thinking Question
Can I add -ed to the verb to show past tense? Does the verb end in e?

Write each sentence using the correct past tense of the verb in parentheses.

1. Evan ________ his parents to send him to cooking school. (want)

   ____

2. We ________ to answer a newspaper ad for a school. (decide)

   ____

3. Many cooking students ________ there. (work)

   ____

4. Evan and I ________ that they would like our letter. (hope)

   ____

5. We ________ the school with the good work we did. (surprise)

   ____

Name ____________________ Date __________

Verbs in the Present

The Extra-good Sunday
Grammar:
Verb Tenses

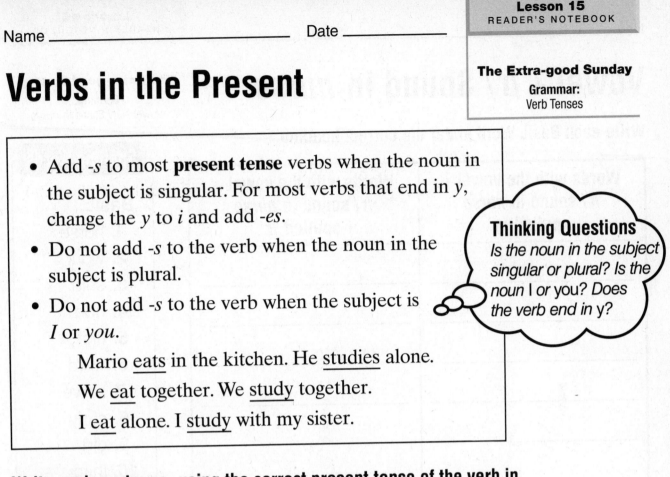

- Add *-s* to most **present tense** verbs when the noun in the subject is singular. For most verbs that end in *y*, change the *y* to *i* and add *-es*.
- Do not add *-s* to the verb when the noun in the subject is plural.
- Do not add *-s* to the verb when the subject is *I* or *you*.

Mario eats in the kitchen. He studies alone.
We eat together. We study together.
I eat alone. I study with my sister.

Thinking Questions
Is the noun in the subject singular or plural? Is the noun I or you? Does the verb end in y?

Write each sentence, using the correct present tense of the verb in parentheses.

1. Uncle Raul ________ a cutting board. (use)

   ____

2. He ________ his tea while we slice onions. (sip)

   ____

3. I _____ when I slice onions. (cry)

   ____

4. Even my dad _____ when he slices onions. (cry)

   ____

Name ____________________ Date __________

Vowel + /r/ Sound in *nurse*

Write each Basic Word under the correct heading.

Words with the vowel + /r/ sound in *nurse* spelled *ur*	Words with the vowel + /r/ sound in *nurse* spelled *ir*
____________	____________
____________	____________
____________	____________
____________	____________
____________	____________
____________	____________
Words with the vowel + /r/ sound in *nurse* spelled *or*	**Words with the vowel + /r/ sound in *nurse* spelled *er***
____________	____________
____________	____________
____________	____________

Spelling Words

Basic

1. nurse
2. work
3. shirt
4. hurt
5. first
6. word
7. serve
8. curly
9. dirt
10. third
11. worry
12. turn
13. stir
14. firm

Review

her
girl

Challenge

perfect
hamburger

Challenge: Which Challenge Word can only be placed in the last box? ____________

Which Challenge Word can be placed in both the first and the last box? ____________

Name ______________________ Date ____________

Focus Trait: Voice

Using Formal Language

Writers change their voice, or how they use their words and language, based on the purpose of their writing. For example, they use formal language with an explanatory essay. Its purpose is to explain.

For example:
Dolphins live in the ocean in groups called pods. They are highly intelligent mammals that communicate through sound, vision, touch, and taste.

The sentences below are written using informal language. Rewrite them using formal language.

1. Tiny monkeys are so cute, and they help people, too!

   ____

2. That police officer is riding a cool bike. He is in a pretty big park.

   ____

   ____

3. I think horses work too hard. They chase cows and carry around people and stuff.

   ____

   ____

4. There's a brush fire! You'd better call 911!

   ____

   ____

Name ______________________ Date __________

Cumulative Review

Write a word from the box to complete each sentence. Then read the sentence.

certainly	herd	working
firmly	turning	burger
spark	report	before

1. This restaurant is known for having a great ______________ and tasty fries.

2. I love to help cook dinner. I think I'm ______________ into a chef!

3. Damon gave a very interesting ______________ about the rain forests.

4. I ______________ don't want to spend all weekend studying.

5. The forest fire began with just a single ______________.

6. Nicole was being silly when she said that she always ate lunch ______________ breakfast.

7. Frank held the ball ______________ as he ran.

8. The cowboys rounded up the ______________ of cattle.

9. Because the dryer is not ______________, my clothes are still wet.

Name ______________________________ Date ______

The Extra-good Sunday

Cooking with Beezus and Ramona

Hi, I am Todd Allen, host of *Cooking at Home!* Beezus and Ramona created a delicious chicken dish for dinner. We are going to find out how they made it!

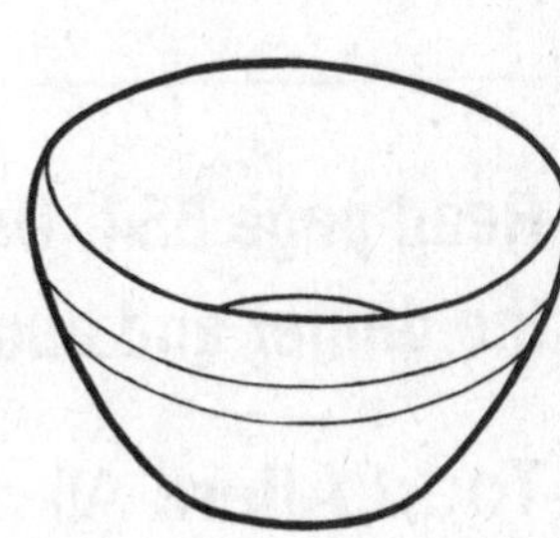

Read pages 543–544 to answer Todd's questions.

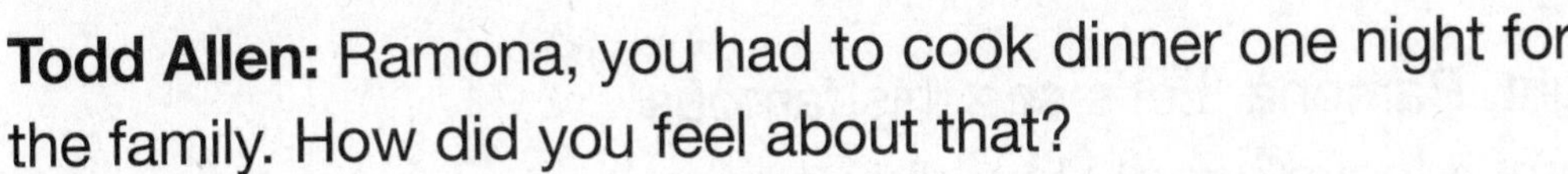

Todd Allen: Ramona, you had to cook dinner one night for the family. How did you feel about that?

Ramona: ______________________________

____

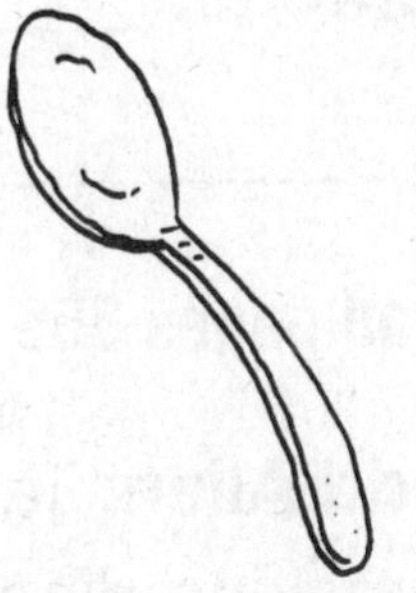

Read page 545 to answer Todd's question.

Todd Allen: Beezus, you wanted to make something awful! Why? What made you change your mind?

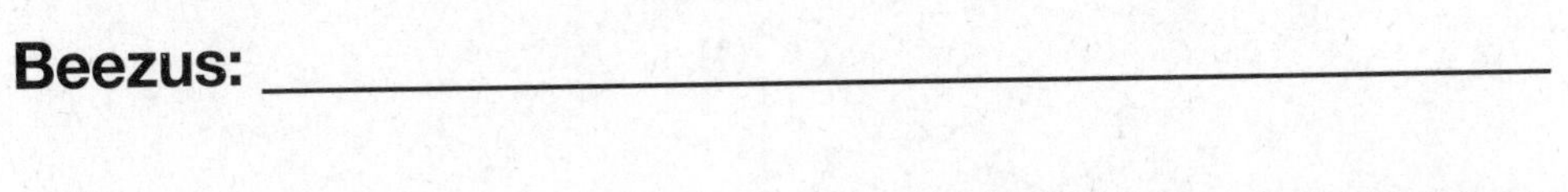

Beezus: ______________________________

____

____

Read pages 546–549 to answer to the next question.

Todd Allen: How did you come up with your special dish?

Ramona: ______________________________

____

____

Name ______________________ Date ______

Read pages 550–552. Use these pages to help Beezus talk about what happened next.

Todd Allen: Beezus, how did you feel about the dinner you were making? Was Ramona helping?

Beezus: ____

____

____

Read page 554. Use this page to help the girls talk about serving the dinner and about their parents' reaction.

Todd Allen: All right, Ramona. Let's see this famous chicken dish. Mmm, it looks good! How did you feel when you brought it out to the table?

Ramona: ____

____

Read pages 555–557. What did Ramona think?

Todd Allen: Tell me, Ramona, what was the best part of making dinner?

Ramona: ____

____

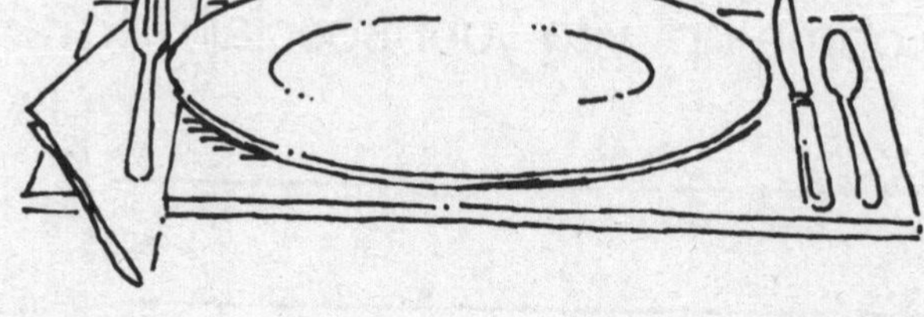

Name ______________________ Date ____________

Verbs in the Future

- A verb that tells about an action that will happen is in the **future tense**.
- Add the word *will* before a verb to form the future tense.

  I will cook the food.

  My family will eat the food.

Write each sentence, using the correct future tense of the verb in parentheses.

1. Theo ________ the recipe cards. (study)

   ____

2. He ________ which recipe to make. (decide)

   ____

3. Doug ________ the chicken. (fry)

   ____

4. Both boys ________ the sauce. (taste)

   ____

5. The younger kids ________ the table. (set)

   ____

6. Theo ________ the meal. (serve)

   ____

Name ______________________ Date ____________

Vowel + /r/ Sound in *nurse*

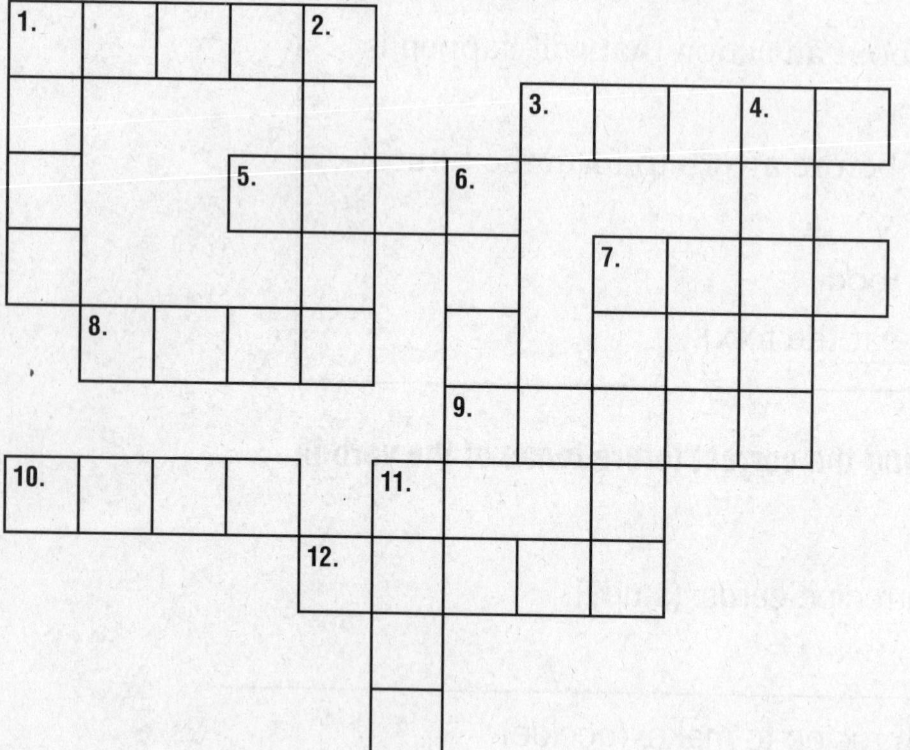

Spelling Words

Basic

1. nurse
2. work
3. shirt
4. hurt
5. first
6. word
7. serve
8. curly
9. dirt
10. third
11. worry
12. turn
13. stir
14. firm

Review

her
girl

Challenge

perfect
hamburger

Use the Basic Words to complete the puzzle.

Across

1. Item of clothing
3. Comes before "second"
5. Soil
7. The opposite of play
8. "Please" is the magic ______.
9. A hospital worker
10. Not soft
12. The opposite of straight

Down

1. To mix
2. Comes after "second"
4. To present or give
6. Move a car right or left
7. Be concerned
11. Injured

Name ______________________ Date ____________

Using a Thesaurus

Read the book review. Look up each underlined word in a thesaurus. Write a synonym for each word.

If you haven't already, you'll want to meet Ramona Quimby. The latest adventures of this special girl appear in *Ramona Quimby, Age 8*. With her father in college and her mother back at work, Ramona has to resolve some things for herself. How will she handle her annoying young neighbor? Will her parents be cross with her when she makes a mess? Will things remain tense with Yard Ape?

There is a reason why Beverly Cleary's books remain some of America's favorites after so many years.

1. ____________________
2. ____________________
3. ____________________
4. ____________________
5. ____________________
6. ____________________

Write two sentences that could be in your own review of *The Extra-good Sunday*. Choose a word in each sentence to look up in a thesaurus and underline it. Write a synonym for that word.

7. ____
8. ____

Name ______________________ Date ____________

Kinds of Pronouns

- A **pronoun** is a word that can take the place of one or more nouns in a sentence. The pronouns *I*, *you*, *he*, *she*, *it*, *we*, and *they* are subject pronouns. Pronouns can be singular or plural.
- The words *me*, *you*, *him*, *her*, *it*, *us*, and *them* are object pronouns. Object pronouns follow action verbs and words like *to*, *for*, *at*, *of*, and *with*.

  Claude did not understand his parents.

  He did not understand them.

Write each sentence. Replace the underlined word or words with a subject or object pronoun.

1. Claude thinks his parents are good people.

   ____

2. Claude shows respect to his parents.

   ____

Replace the repeated noun in these sentences with a pronoun. Write the new sentences on the lines.

3. Claude loves to eat. Claude enjoys eating with his family.

   ____

4. Claude loves his friends. His friends see him every day.

   ____

Name ____________________ Date __________

The Extra-good Sunday
Spelling:
Vowel + /r/ Sound in *nurse*

Proofread for Spelling

Circle the ten misspelled Spelling Words in this diary entry. Then write each word correctly.

June 2nd

Today was the purfect day. Dad decided to take a day off from wirk, and we went to the baseball game. Our seats were on the ferst base side of the field. The grass looked so green, and the durt on the infield looked so soft. As we sat down, Dad smiled and asked if my hair was getting more cirly. Before I could say a wurd, I saw my favorite player. He is the therd baseman, and he wears number 20 on his shurt. That's my favorite number, too! The last time we came to a game, he was hirt, but he was healthy today. Dad ordered me a hambirgur, and we settled in to watch a great game.

1. ____________ 6. ____________

2. ____________ 7. ____________

3. ____________ 8. ____________

4. ____________ 9. ____________

5. ____________ 10. ____________

Spelling Words

Basic

1. nurse
2. work
3. shirt
4. hurt
5. first
6. word
7. serve
8. curly
9. dirt
10. third
11. worry
12. turn
13. stir
14. firm

Review

her
girl

Challenge

perfect
hamburger

Name ______________________ Date ____________

Connect to Writing

Using incorrect verb tenses in your writing can confuse the reader. Use the correct verb tense to show when actions happen. Remember to use the correct verb endings or the word *will* before the verb.

Present Tense	Past Tense	Future Tense
I talk.	I talked.	I will talk.
She talks.	She talked.	She will talk.
They talk.	They talked.	They will talk.

Choose the correct tense for each sentence. Write the verb.

1. The family (cooked, will cook) breakfast together. (future tense)

____

2. Dad (mixes, mixed) the pancake batter in a bowl. (past tense)

____

3. Harry (pours, will pour) the batter in the pan. (present tense)

____

4. When the pancakes are ready, Harry (flipped, will flip) them. (future tense)

____

5. Mom, Dad, and Harry (enjoy, will enjoy) their breakfast. (present tense)

____